Delia

SMITH'S

WINTER COLLECTION

Illustrations by Flo Bayley

TED SMART

DEDICATION

To everyone at The Magazine,
thank you for your patience

—————————— ◇ ——————————

This book is published to accompany the television series entitled
Delia Smith's Winter Collection which was first
broadcast in October 1995.
Executive Producer Frances Whitaker
Produced and directed by Trevor Hampton

This edition produced for
The Book People Ltd,
Hall Wood Avenue, Haydock,
St Helens WA11 9UL
by BBC Books,
an imprint of BBC Worldwide Publishing.
BBC Worldwide Ltd, Woodlands,
80 Wood Lane, London W12 0TT

First published in this edition 2000
© Delia Smith 1995
The moral right of the author has been asserted

ISBN 1 85613 759 7

Illustrations by Flo Bayley
All photographs by Peter Knab, except the following:
Jean Cazals (page 93), Tony Heathcote (page 56),
Norman Hollands (pages 129; 196–7), Kevin Summers (pages 17; 32;
80; 84; 116; 120–121; 136–7; 156; 216–17).

Set in Monotype Baskerville
Printed and bound in Great Britain by Butler & Tanner Ltd, Frome, Somerset
Colour separation by Radstock Reproductions, Midsomer Norton
Jacket printed by Lawrence Allen Ltd, Weston-super-Mare

My thanks to
Mary Cox, Catherine Calland, Lulu Grimes and Tamsin Burnett-Hall
for their help with the recipe testing, photography and TV series.
To Jane Houghton for co-ordinating the book and to Diana Hughes,
Aggie MacKenzie and Eirwen Hughes for their help with the production.
My thanks also to Kevin Summers, Norman Hollands, Jean Cazals and
Tony Heathcote for allowing me to include their splendid photographs from
Sainsbury's The Magazine and a special thanks to Peter Knab who beautifully
photographed the rest of this book and to Flo Bayley for the lovely drawings.

CONTENTS

Conversion Tables

All these are approximate conversions, which have either been rounded up or down. In a few recipes it has been necessary to modify them very slightly. Never mix metric and imperial measures in one recipe, stick to one system or the other. All spoon measurements used throughout this book are level unless specified otherwise.

Oven temperatures

Gas Mark	°F	°C
1	275	140
2	300	150
3	325	170
4	350	180
5	375	190
6	400	200
7	425	220
8	450	230
9	475	240

Measurements

1/8 inch	3	mm
1/4	5	mm
1/2	1	cm
3/4	2	
1	2.5	
1 1/4	3	
1 1/2	4	
1 3/4	4.5	
2	5	
2 1/2	6	
3	7.5	
3 1/2	9	
4	10	
5	13	
5 1/4	13.5	
6	15	
6 1/2	16	
7	18	
7 1/2	19	
8	20	
9	23	
9 1/2	24	
10	25.5	
11	28	
12	30	

Weights

1/2 oz	10 g
3/4	20
1	25
1 1/2	40
2	50
2 1/2	60
3	75
4	110
4 1/2	125
5	150
6	175
7	200
8	225
9	250
10	275
12	350
1 lb	450
1 1/2	700
2	900
3	1.35 kg

Volume

2 fl oz	55 ml
3	75
5 (1/4 pt)	150
1/2 pt	275
1	570
1 1/4	725
1 3/4	1 litre
2	1.2
2 1/2	1.5
4	2.25

Introduction

E ver since I was a small child I have felt a sense of magic in the changing Seasons. For me this sense of change and the fact that nothing ever remains quite the same gives our everyday life that joyful quality of anticipation. Having said that, I can envisage nods of agreement when it comes to Spring or Summer.........but Winter? Perhaps a few furrowed brows?

The truth is that Winter has every bit as much charm as the other seasons for me: the dazzling splendour of autumnal colours and Keats' as yet unmatched description of mists and mellow fruitfulness, the stark emptiness of bare branches against the Winter skies, and always the very special pale Winter light.

Yes, there will be cold and grey days and long dark nights, but surely it is in Winter that food comes into our lives with an even sharper focus – because it's then that we all need to be warm, cosy and comforted. In Winter cooking and eating is a much more serious affair – and here on the following pages I have attempted to offer what I hope is a strong case for reviving this idea.

I have an instinct (no more), that perhaps our current preoccupation with healthy eating has eclipsed what I consider to be a very health-giving joy of more traditional cooking, of eating gathered round a table enjoying conversation, good food and good wine.

OK. excesses of anything are unhealthy. I'm not suggesting you eat Steak and Kidney pudding followed by Fallen Chocolate Soufflé every day, but what I am saying is let's not completely lose sight of our heritage: puddings steaming merrily on the stove, the smell of home baking and the evocative aroma and the sound of a joint sizzling in the oven after a long frosty walk. Then there's that glorious anticipation of something braising long and slow whilst at the same time all its wonderful flavours are being gently imparted.

I could of course go on and on, but now it's over to you – and hopefully as you read and try the recipes you too will share my enthusiasm and joy in all that Winter cooking has to offer.

Delia Smith

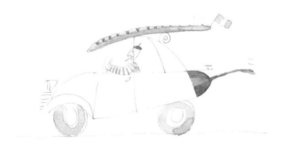

CHAPTER ONE

W ARMING UP –
the
SOUP COLLECTION

———— ◇ ————

A lthough there are some delightful summer versions, it's during the winter months that soups really come into their own. Steaming bowls of something fragrant and home-made are not just psychologically warming, they're physically warming too. Like nothing else hot soup really does give you an inner glow right down to the chilliest fingers and toes. So it's been essential for me to find and put together a very special collection of home-made winter soups to begin this book. If I'm honest I was apprehensive at the prospect of doing this as, looking back over the years, I seemed to have already made every soup in existence. But what I want people to know is that the whole subject of food and cooking never loses its fresh edge; new ideas are always popping up through travel, friends and discovering new ingredients. And the result is nine of the best soups I've ever tasted – I know you won't be disappointed!

Most of the following recipes have two dimensions. First, on their own they are good for large family meals along with good bread, cheese and salad. Secondly, with the addition of an interesting garnish, you have something a little more special for entertaining.

Stocks are now available in tubs from supermarkets, but if you need a large quantity these can be expensive. Powdered vegetable stock, gluten-free, is made by a company called Marigold and is available from health food shops – an excellent store cupboard standby. For those who do not have my other books, here's how to make vegetable stock and chicken stock – either of which can be used for the soups in this chapter – and a choice of croûtons.

————————

Quick Vegetable Stock

1 stick of celery, cut in half and split lengthways	12 black peppercorns
2 small carrots, split in half lengthways	1 small bunch of parsley stalks and celery leaves
2 small onions, sliced	Salt
2 bay leaves	1–1½ pints (570–850 ml) cold water

Simply place all the ingredients in a saucepan, cover it with a lid, bring everything to the boil, and boil briskly for 30 minutes. After that strain, discarding the vegetables, and the stock is ready for use.

◇

Chicken Giblet Stock

1 set of chicken giblets (or see below)	12 black peppercorns
1 stick of celery, cut in half and split lengthways	1 small bunch of parsley stalks and celery leaves
2 small carrots, split lengthways	Salt
2 small onions, sliced	2 pints (1.2 litres) cold water
2 bay leaves	

Place the giblets and the rest of the ingredients in a saucepan, cover and bring to the boil. Boil it briskly for 1 hour, then strain, discarding the giblets and vegetables. If you can't get hold of chicken giblets, use a couple of chicken wing tips instead.

◇

Croûtons

SERVES 4

2 oz (50 g) bread cut into small cubes
1 tablespoon olive oil

Pre-heat the oven to gas mark 4, 350°F (180°C).

Just place the cubes of bread in a bowl together with the oil, and stir them around so that they get an even coating. Then arrange them on a baking sheet.

Bake them on a high shelf in the oven for 10 minutes or until they are crisp and golden. One word of warning: do use a kitchen timer for this operation because it's actually very hard to bake something for just 10 minutes without forgetting all about it. I have baked more batches of charcoal-coloured croûtons than I care to remember! Then allow them to cool, and leave them on one side until the soup is ready or store them in a screw-top jar.

———————— ◇ ————————

Garlic Croûtons

Follow the recipe above, only this time add 1 crushed clove of garlic to the bowl along with the olive oil and cubes of bread.

———————— ◇ ————————

Parmesan Croûtons

For this you place the oil and cubes of bread in a small bowl, stir them around until the oil is soaked up, then sprinkle in 1 dessertspoon of freshly grated Parmesan. Stir the cubes around to coat them in that as well, then spread them on the baking sheet and bake as above.

———————— ◇ ————————

Chickpea, Chilli and Coriander Soup

SERVES 4–6

This has decidedly Mexican overtones. It isn't too hot and spicy but the presence of the chilli does give it a nice kick, and the flavour and texture of chickpeas is perfect for soup.

8 oz (225 g) chickpeas, soaked overnight in twice their volume of cold water	2–3 tablespoons lemon juice
2 oz (50 g) butter	1 x 15 g pack (or ½ oz) fresh coriander, leaves and stalks separated
1 level tablespoon coriander seeds	1 x 200 ml tub crème fraîche
1 level tablespoon cumin seeds	Salt and freshly milled black pepper
6 fat cloves garlic, peeled and finely chopped	FOR THE GARNISH:
2 small red chillies, halved, de-seeded and chopped	1 mild, fat red or green chilli, de-seeded and cut into very fine hair-like shreds
1 level teaspoon ground turmeric	
Grated zest of 1 lemon	

You will also need a large saucepan of 6-pint (3.5-litre) capacity.

First of all drain the chickpeas in a colander, rinse them under the cold tap then place them in the saucepan with 2½ pints (1.5 litres) of boiling unsalted water. Then bring them up to simmering point, put a lid on and cook them very gently for about 1 hour or until the chickpeas are absolutely tender and squashy.

While they're cooking prepare the rest of the soup ingredients. The coriander and cumin seeds should be dry-roasted in a small pre-heated pan for 2–3 minutes, then crushed in a pestle and mortar. After that melt the butter in the pan, add the crushed spices along with the chopped garlic and chillies and cook over a low heat for about 5 minutes. Now add the turmeric, stir and heat that gently before removing the pan from the heat.

As soon as the chickpeas are tender, drain them in a colander placed over a bowl to reserve the cooking water. Transfer the chickpeas to a liquidizer together with a couple of ladles of cooking water and purée them until fine and smooth. Now add the lemon zest, coriander stalks and spices from the pan along with another ladleful of cooking water and blend once more until fine and smooth.

Next the whole lot needs to go back into the saucepan with the rest of the reserved cooking water. Bring it all up to a gentle simmer, give it a good stir, season, then simmer gently for a further 30 minutes. All this can be done in advance, then when you're ready to serve the soup re-heat very gently without letting it come to the boil. Stir in half the crème fraîche and the lemon juice, taste to check the seasoning, then serve in hot soup bowls with the rest of the crème fraîche swirled in and scatter with the shredded chilli and coriander leaves as a garnish.

––––––––––––– ◇ –––––––––––––

Next page: Roasted Pumpkin Soup with Melting Cheese (see page 14)

Roasted Pumpkin Soup with Melting Cheese

SERVES 6

*T*he lovely thing about pumpkin is that it has a really velvety texture in soup, and if it's oven-roasted before you add it to the soup, it gives an unusual nuttiness to the flavour. Just before serving, add little cubes of quick melting cheese like Gruyère or, if you're lucky enough to get it, Fontina. Then finding little bits of half-melted cheese in the soup that stretch up on the spoon is an absolute delight. (See photograph on pages 12–13.)

1 pumpkin weighing 3–3½ lb (1.35–1.6 kg)
1 tablespoon groundnut oil
1 large onion, peeled and finely chopped
1½ pints (850 ml) stock, vegetable or chicken
15 fl oz (425 ml) whole milk
1 oz (25 g) butter
Freshly grated nutmeg
Salt and freshly milled black pepper

TO SERVE:
4 oz (110 g) Gruyère or Fontina, cut into ¼-inch (5-mm) dice
2 oz (50 g) Gruyère or Fontina, coarsely grated
6 teaspoons crème fraîche
Croûtons (see page 10)
Flat-leaf parsley

You will also need a solid baking sheet that won't buckle in the high heat, and a 6-pint (3.5-litre) saucepan.

Pre-heat the oven to gas mark 9, 475°F (240°C).

Begin by cutting the pumpkin in half through the stalk, then cut each half into 4 again and scoop out the seeds using a large spoon. Then brush the surface of each section with the oil and place them on the baking sheet. Season with salt and pepper, then pop them on a high shelf of the oven to roast for 25–30 minutes or until tender when tested with a skewer.

Meanwhile melt the butter in a large saucepan over a high heat, add the onion, stir it round and when it begins to colour around the edges, after about 5 minutes, turn the heat down. Let it cook very gently without a lid, giving it a stir from time to time, for about 20 minutes.

Then remove the pumpkin from the oven and leave it aside to cool. Now add the stock and the milk to the onions, and leave them with the heat turned low to slowly come up to simmering point. Next scoop out the flesh of the pumpkin with a sharp knife and add it to the stock together with a seasoning of salt, pepper and nutmeg. Then let it all simmer very gently for about 15–20 minutes.

Next the soup should be processed to a purée. Because there's a large volume of soup, it's best to do this in two halves. What you need to do is whizz it until it's smoothly blended, but as an extra precaution it's best to pass it through a sieve as well in case there are any unblended fibrous bits. Taste and season well, then when you're ready to serve the soup re-heat it gently just up to simmering point, being careful not to let it boil.

Finally, stir in the diced cheese, then ladle the soup into warm soup bowls. Garnish each bowl with a teaspoonful of crème fraîche and scatter with the grated cheese, a few croûtons as well, if you like them, and a sprinkling of parsley.

Polish Beetroot Soup

SERVES 4

Beetroot is either loved or hated – mostly the latter I suspect, because in this country people have a surfeit of it doused in strong vinegar. But its lovers know of its earthy charm and delicious but distinctive flavour. It makes wonderful soup, and this one is Polish in origin and especially good. Although the soup is a dazzling colour, you won't want your hands to match it, so it's best to wear gloves while you're handling it!

FOR THE STOCK:	FOR THE SOUP:
6 oz (175 g) belly pork cut in cubes	**1½ lb (700 g) uncooked beetroot, whole but with stalks removed**
1 large carrot, cut in chunks	
1 medium onion, roughly chopped	**1 level tablespoon plain flour, mixed to a paste with 1 oz (25 g) butter**
1 bay leaf	
A handful of parsley stalks	**5 fl oz (150 ml) soured cream**
1 dessertspoon of oil	**2 tablespoons lemon juice**
2 pints (1.2 litres) water	**Salt**
Salt and freshly milled black pepper	

You will also need a large saucepan of about 6-pint (3.5-litre) capacity.

First of all you need to make a stock: heat the oil in a large saucepan and when it's really hot, brown the pieces of pork, carrot and onion, keeping the heat high so they turn brownish-black at the edges. This is important because it gives the stock a good flavour.

When you're happy with the colour (after about 6 minutes) add the water, bay leaf and parsley stalks, followed by a good seasoning of salt and freshly milled pepper. As soon as it begins to simmer turn the heat down and let it simmer very gently without a lid for 40 minutes. After that strain it through a sieve into a bowl, throw out the stock ingredients and rinse the saucepan to use again.

While the stock is cooking you can deal with the beetroot. Place it in another saucepan, add enough boiling water to just cover, then add salt. Put on a lid and simmer gently for 40 minutes or until tender when pierced with a skewer. After that drain off the water, then cover the beetroot with cold water to cool it down. As soon as it's cool enough to handle, take off the skin. Now reserve one beetroot (about 4 oz, 110 g) for the garnish and cut the rest into cubes. Next transfer it to the saucepan in which you made the stock, add the stock, bring to simmering point, cover and simmer gently for 20 minutes.

Now, using a draining spoon, transfer the beetroot to a liquidizer or food processor, put the lid on, switch on the motor and whilst it's running add the flour and butter paste, the soup stock followed by 3 fl oz (75 ml) of soured cream. When it's all blended pour it back into the saucepan, add the lemon juice, taste to check the seasoning and re-heat very gently, without letting it come to the boil. Grate the reserved beetroot on the fine side of the grater. Then serve the soup in warmed soup bowls, swirl in the remaining soured cream and scatter the grated beetroot on top as a garnish. For entertaining, croûtons (see page 10) made with black rye bread would be a good addition.

Curried Parsnip and Apple Soup with Parsnip Crisps

SERVES 6

This is such a lovely soup. The sweetness of the parsnips is sharpened by the presence of the apple, and the subtle flavour of the spices comes through beautifully. If you're entertaining, the soup can be enhanced by some crunchy parsnip crisps sprinkled over as a garnish (see right).

1½ lb (700 g) young parsnips	1 heaped teaspoon cumin seeds
1½ oz (40 g) butter	6 whole cardamom pods, seeds only
1 tablespoon groundnut oil	1 heaped teaspoon turmeric
2 medium onions, chopped	1 heaped teaspoon ground ginger
2 cloves garlic, chopped	Salt and freshly milled black pepper
2 pints (1.2 litres) good flavoured stock (see page 9)	
1 medium Bramley apple (6 oz, 175 g)	
1 heaped teaspoon coriander seeds	

You will also need a large saucepan of about 6-pint (3.5-litre) capacity.

Begin by heating a small frying pan and dry-roasting the coriander, cumin and cardamom seeds – this is to toast them and draw out their flavour. After 2–3 minutes they will change colour and start to jump in the pan. Remove them from the pan and crush them finely with a pestle and mortar.

Next heat the butter and oil in a saucepan until the butter begins to foam, then add the onions and gently soften for about 5 minutes before adding the garlic. Let that cook along with the onions for another 2 minutes, then add all the crushed spices along with the turmeric and ginger, stir and let it all continue to cook gently for a few more minutes while you peel and chop the parsnips into 1-inch (2.5-cm) dice. Add the parsnips to the saucepan, stirring well, then pour in the stock, add some seasoning and let the soup simmer as gently as possible for 1 hour without putting on a lid.

After that remove it from the heat, then liquidize it if possible; if not, use a food processor and then a sieve – or even just a sieve, squashing the ingredients through using the bowl of a ladle. After the soup has been puréed return it to the saucepan, taste to check the seasoning, then when you're ready to serve re-heat very gently. While that's happening, peel the apple and as the soup just reaches simmering point grate the apple into it. Be careful to let the soup barely simmer for only 3–4 minutes. Serve in hot soup bowls garnished with parsnip crisps.

◇

Parsnip Crisps

1 medium to large parsnip **(10–12 oz, 275–350 g)**	**6 tablespoons groundnut oil** **Salt**

First peel the parsnip and then slice it into rounds as thinly as you possibly can, using a sharp knife. Now heat the oil in a 10-inch (25.5-cm) frying pan until it is very hot, almost smoking, then fry the parsnip slices in batches until they are golden brown, about 2–3 minutes (they will not stay flat or colour evenly but will twist into lovely shapes). As they're cooked remove them with a slotted spoon and spread them out on kitchen paper to drain. Sprinkle lightly with salt. If you like you can make these in advance as they will stay crisp for a couple of hours.

◇

Black Bean Soup with Black Bean Salsa

SERVES 4–6

*T*his soup is simply stunning, one you'll want to make over and over again. Black beans don't have a strong flavour of their own but they do carry other flavours superbly, while at the same time yielding a unique velvety texture. If you forget to soak the beans overnight, bring them up to the boil for 10 minutes and then pre-soak them for three hours. Serving salsa with soup makes a clever contrast of the cold refreshing textures of the vegetables and the hot lusciousness of the soup.

9 oz (250 g) black beans
1 x 70 g pack (or 3 oz) pancetta, or smoked bacon, finely chopped
1 large onion, chopped small
2 oz (50 g) carrot, chopped small
2 oz (50 g) swede, chopped small
1 fat clove garlic, crushed
1 teaspoon cumin seeds
1 teaspoon Tabasco sauce
1 x 15 g pack (or ½ oz) coriander, stalks finely chopped and leaves reserved for the salsa
2 pints (1.2 litres) chicken stock
2 tablespoons olive oil
Salt and freshly milled black pepper
1 heaped tablespoon crème fraîche

Juice of ½ lime (keep other ½ for the salsa)

FOR THE SALSA:

3 large spoons cooked beans – see method
2 large tomatoes, not too ripe
1 small red onion, finely chopped
1 green chilli, de-seeded and chopped
Coriander leaves reserved from above
1 dessertspoon extra virgin olive oil
Juice of ½ lime
Salt and freshly milled black pepper

You will also need a large saucepan of about 6-pint (3.5-litre) capacity.

It's best to start the soup the night before by throwing the beans into a pan and covering them with approximately twice their volume of cold water. Next day, drain them in a colander and rinse them under a cold running tap. Now take the saucepan and heat the 2 tablespoons of olive oil. As soon as it's really hot, add the chopped pancetta and cook for about 5 minutes. Then turn the heat down to medium, stir in the onion, garlic, carrot, swede and coriander stalks and continue to cook for another 10 minutes with the lid on, stirring everything round once or twice.

While that's happening heat a small frying pan over a medium heat, then add the cumin seeds and dry-roast them for 2–3 minutes until they become very aromatic, begin to change colour and start to dance in the pan. At that point remove them from the pan and crush them to a coarse powder with a pestle and mortar. Add this to the vegetables along with the drained beans, Tabasco sauce and stock (but no salt at this stage), then bring everything up to a gentle simmer for about 1½ hours with the lid on. It's very important to keep the simmer as gentle as possible, so you might need to use a heat diffuser here.

When the time is up, use a slotted spoon to remove 3 rounded spoonfuls of the beans, rinse and drain them in a sieve and reserve them for the salsa. Now you need to purée the soup and the best way to do this is in a liquidizer – if not, a processor and a sieve will do or even just a sieve. When the soup is liquidized, return it to the saucepan, add the lime juice, season with salt and pepper and it's now ready for re-heating later when you want to serve it.

TO MAKE THE SALSA

Pour boiling water over the tomatoes, leave them for 1 minute, then slip the skins off, cut them in half and gently squeeze each half in your hand to remove the seeds. After the seeds are removed, chop the tomato into small dice and place it in a bowl along with the reserved beans, the finely chopped red onion, green chilli, coriander leaves and the extra virgin olive oil. Then add the juice of half a lime, some salt and freshly milled black pepper and leave it aside for about 1 hour for the flavours to mingle and be absorbed.

To serve the soup, re-heat it very gently, being careful not to allow it to come to the boil, as boiling always spoils the flavour of soup. Serve in warm soup bowls, adding a spoonful of crème fraîche and an equal portion of salsa sprinkled over the surface.

If you're entertaining and really want to have some fun, make this soup *and* the White Bean Soup on page 22, and serve them together with one or other of the garnishes. All you do is re-heat both soups, then using two ladles pour both ladlefuls into the warmed bowls simultaneously, one from the left, the other from the right. It works a treat (see photograph on page 20) and makes a lovely contrast. Any leftover soup can be frozen.

————————◇————————

Next page: Black Bean Soup and Tuscan White Bean Soup (see page 22)

Smoked Haddock Chowder with Poached Eggs

SERVES 4

*S*moked haddock makes a very fine soup, and this I've adapted from a famous version invented in Scotland where it is called Cullen skink. If you add poached quails' eggs to the soup this makes a delightful surprise as you lift up an egg on your spoon. For a main course meal you could use poached hens' eggs to make it more substantial. Either way it is lovely served with brown bread and butter.

1 lb 4 oz (560 g) undyed smoked haddock, cut into 4 pieces	1 tablespoon lemon juice
18 fl oz (500 ml) milk	8 quails' eggs (or 4 hens' eggs)
18 fl oz (500 ml) water	1 tablespoon chopped flat-leaf parsley
1 bay leaf	Salt and freshly milled black pepper
1½ oz (40 g) butter	
1 medium onion, finely chopped	
1 oz (25 g) flour	

You will also need a large saucepan of about 6-pint (3.5-litre) capacity, and 4 warmed shallow soup bowls.

Start off by placing the haddock pieces in a large saucepan, pour in the milk and water, season with pepper (but no salt yet) and add the bay leaf. Now gently bring it up to simmering point and simmer very gently for 5 minutes before taking it off the heat and pouring it all into a bowl to steep for 15 minutes.

Meanwhile, wipe the saucepan with kitchen paper and melt the butter, add the chopped onion and let it sweat very gently without browning for about 10 minutes. By that time the haddock will be ready, so remove it with a draining spoon (reserving the liquid) to a board, discard the bay leaf and peel off the skin.

Next stir the flour into the pan to soak up the juices, then gradually add the fish-cooking liquid, stirring after each addition. When that's all in, add half the haddock separated into flakes.

Now pour the soup into a liquidizer or food processor and blend thoroughly. After that pass it through a sieve back into the saucepan, pressing any solid bits of haddock that are left to extract all the flavour. Discard what's left in the sieve then separate the remaining haddock into flakes and add these to the soup. Taste it now and season with salt, pepper and lemon juice and leave to one side to keep warm.

Now poach the eggs: pour boiling water straight into a medium-sized frying pan and place over a heat gentle enough for there to be the merest trace of bubbles simmering on the base of the pan. Break the 8 quails' eggs (or 4 hens' eggs) into the water and let them cook for just 1 minute. Then remove the pan from the heat and let the quails' eggs stand in the water for 3 minutes, and the hens' eggs for 10, after which time the whites will be set and the yolks creamy. Use a draining spoon and a wad of kitchen paper underneath to remove the eggs, place 2 quails' eggs (or one hen's egg) in each warmed serving bowl, ladle the soup on top and serve sprinkled with the chopped parsley.

Libyan Soup with Couscous

SERVES 6

This recipe first appeared in 'The Food Aid Cookery Book', published in 1986. Its con-tributor Mary El-Rayes has kindly given me permission to reprint it here. It's a truly wonderful soup, meaty with lots of fragrant flavour, and perfect for serving on a really cold winter's day with pitta bread warm from the oven.

6 oz (175 g) finely chopped raw lamb, leg steak or similar	**4 oz (110 g) dried chickpeas (soaked overnight in twice their volume of cold water)**
1 heaped teaspoon coriander seeds	**2 oz (50 g) couscous**
1 heaped teaspoon cumin seeds	**1 tablespoon chopped fresh parsley**
1 large onion, peeled and chopped	**1 tablespoon chopped fresh mint**
2 cloves garlic, peeled and crushed with 1 level teaspoon sea salt in a pestle and mortar	**2 tablespoons oil**
	Salt to taste
1 heaped teaspoon ground allspice	
2 heaped teaspoons mild chilli powder	TO SERVE:
1 x 140 g tin tomato purée	**Pitta bread**
1 green chilli, de-seeded and chopped	**Lemon wedges**
2 teaspoons caster sugar	
1½ pints (850 ml) water	You will also need a large saucepan of about 6-pint (3.5-litre) capacity with a well-fitting lid.
1 pint (570 ml) good lamb stock	

Begin by pre-heating a small frying pan over a medium heat, then add the coriander and cumin seeds and dry-roast them for about 2–3 minutes, moving them around the pan until they change colour and begin to dance. This will draw out their full spicy flavour. Now crush them quite finely with a pestle and mortar.

Next heat 1 tablespoon of the oil in the saucepan and gently cook the onion until soft and lightly browned, about 5 or 6 minutes, then add the crushed garlic and let that cook for another 2 minutes. After that add the crushed spices, the allspice and chilli powder and stir them into the juices in the pan. Now transfer all this to a plate and keep it aside while you heat the other tablespoon of oil in the same pan until it's very hot. Then add the pieces of lamb and brown them, quickly turning them over and keeping them on the move.

Turn the heat down and now return the onion and spice mixture to the pan to join the meat, adding the tomato purée, chopped chilli and caster sugar. Stir everything together, then add the water and stock. Give it all another good stir then drain the soaked chickpeas, discarding their soaking liquid, and add these to the pan. Give a final stir then put a lid on and simmer as gently as possible for 1 hour or until the chickpeas are tender.

When you're ready to serve the soup taste it, add some salt, then add the couscous, parsley and mint and take the pan off the heat. Put the lid back on and let it stand for 3 minutes before serving in hot soup bowls. Serve with lemon wedges to squeeze into the soup and some warm pitta bread.

French Onion Soup (see page 26)

French Onion Soup

SERVES 6

There are few things more comforting than making a real *French Onion Soup* – slowly cooked caramelized onions that turn mellow and sweet in a broth laced with white wine and Cognac. The whole thing is finished off with crunchy baked croûtons of crusty bread topped with melted, toasted cheese. If ever there was a winter stomach warmer, this is surely it! (See photograph on page 25.)

1½ lb (700 g) onions, thinly sliced	FOR THE CROUTONS:
2 tablespoons olive oil	**French bread or *baguettine*, cut into**
2 oz (50 g) butter	**1-inch (2.5-cm) diagonal slices**
2 cloves garlic, crushed	**1 tablespoon olive oil**
½ teaspoon granulated sugar	**1–2 cloves garlic, crushed**
2 pints (1.2 litres) good beef stock	
10 fl oz (275 ml) dry white wine	TO SERVE:
2 tablespoons Cognac	**6 large or 12 small croûtons**
Salt and freshly milled black pepper	**8 oz (225 g) Gruyère, grated**

Pre-heat the oven to gas mark 4, 350°F (180°C).

You will also need a heavy based saucepan or flameproof casserole of 6-pint (3.5-litre) capacity and a heatproof tureen or soup bowls.

First make the croûtons – begin by drizzling the olive oil on a large, solid baking sheet, add the crushed garlic and, then, using your hands, spread the oil and garlic all over the baking sheet. Now place the bread slices on top of the oil, then turn over each one so that both sides have been lightly coated with the oil. Bake for 20–25 minutes till crisp and crunchy.

Next place the saucepan or casserole on a high heat and melt the oil and butter together. When this is very hot, add the onions, garlic and sugar, and keep turning them from time to time until the edges of the onions have turned dark – this will take about 6 minutes. Then reduce the heat to its lowest setting and leave the onions to carry on cooking very slowly for about 30 minutes, by which time the base of the pan will be covered with a rich, nut brown, caramelized film.

After that pour in the stock and white wine, season, then stir with a wooden spoon, scraping the base of the pan well. As soon as it all comes up to simmering point, turn down the heat to its lowest setting, then go away and leave it to cook very gently, without a lid, for about 1 hour.

All this can be done in advance, but when you're ready to serve the soup, bring it back up to simmering point, taste to check for seasoning – and if it's extra-cold outside, add a couple of tablespoons of Cognac! Warm the tureen or soup bowls in a low oven and pre-heat the grill to its highest setting. Then ladle in the hot soup and top with the croûtons, allowing them to float on the top of the soup.

Now sprinkle the grated Gruyère thickly over the croûtons and place the whole lot under the grill until the cheese is golden brown and bubbling. Serve immediately – and don't forget to warn your guests that everything is very hot!

CHAPTER TWO

———————————◇———————————

WARM SALADS, HOT STARTERS *and* SUPPER DISHES

———————◇———————

Winter salads have become much more popular in recent years, mainly due to the improving quality of imported salad vegetables. There was a time when these were limp and tasteless, but now they're getting better and better all the time. For instance our English Fenland Celery Growers move their whole operation to Spain during the winter to provide us with crisp and crunchy celery all year round. There is also a dazzling array of salad leaves constantly winging their way to us from around the world, not to mention fresh herbs and an enormous choice of vinegars and oils.

What is also helpful in winter is the current fashion for warm salads, where some of the ingredients are warm or even hot but the crisp fresh texture of the salad is retained. Most of the hot starters included in this chapter can double up as supper dishes serving fewer people.

If you are entertaining you may like to consider other starters elsewhere in the book. There are dishes that translate easily from lunch to evening meal in almost every chapter: try Linguini with Mussels and Walnut Parsley Pesto (page 66), Fillets of Sole Véronique (page 49), Oven-Baked Wild Mushroom Risotto (page 101), Red Onion Tarte Tatin (page 94), Roasted and Sun-Dried Tomato Risotto (page 99), Warm Roquefort Cheesecake with Pears in Balsamic Vinaigrette (page 92), Pancake Cannelloni with Spinach and Four Cheeses (page 89), Mashed Black-Eyed Beancakes with Ginger Onion Marmalade (page 104).

———————

Pan-Roasted Italian Onions with San Daniele Ham and Shaved Pecorino

SERVES 4 AS A STARTER

I first tasted this at one of my favourite London restaurants, Le Caprice, and loved it so much I asked for the recipe, which the chefs Mark Hix and Tim Hughes very kindly gave me. It is really one of the nicest first courses I have ever had. San Daniele is available from specialist food shops but if you can't get hold of it use thinly sliced Parma ham. And the same applies to the sheep's cheese Pecorino, which can be replaced by Parmigiano Reggiano.

12 oz (350 g) flat Italian onions or shallots, peeled	**1 teaspoon thyme leaves**
6–8 oz (175–225 g) San Daniele ham, thinly sliced	**2 fl oz (55 ml) balsamic vinegar**
4 oz (110 g) mature Pecorino Romano	**Salt and coarsely crushed peppercorns**
2 fl oz (55 ml) extra virgin olive oil	
1 teaspoon brown sugar	

Begin by heating the olive oil in a thick-based saucepan, stir in the onions or shallots, cover and cook over a medium heat for 5 minutes. After that add the brown sugar, thyme leaves, the salt and pepper and 2 tablespoons water. Cover the pan and cook slowly over a low heat – stirring the onions from time to time to prevent them sticking to the base of the pan – for about 30–35 minutes or until the liquid caramelizes slightly and the onions are soft, with a little colour.

After that, add the balsamic vinegar to the pan, stir well then remove it straight away from the heat, and allow the onions to cool (if you want to prepare this part in advance you can store them at this stage in an airtight jar in the fridge).

Just before you are ready to serve, pre-heat the oven to gas mark 4, 350°F (180°C) and place the onions in a shallow, lidded casserole for 15 minutes. After that arrange them on a plate with a little of the balsamic dressing spooned over. Lay the ham over the onions and use a potato peeler to shave the Pecorino over it. Now spoon a little more of the dressing around the plate and sprinkle some crushed black pepper over the cheese. Serve with ciabatta and some good butter.

——————— ◇ ———————

Baked Eggs in Wild Mushroom Tartlets

SERVES 6 AS A STARTER

*I*t's quite a long time since I made a large quiche or tart for entertaining. I feel that serving them individually is prettier and more practical, and people seem to really enjoy them. This recipe contains a base of a very concentrated mixture of fresh mushrooms and dried porcini, and this is a delight coupled with a softly baked egg and crisp pastry. (See photograph on page 32.)

FOR THE PASTRY:

3 oz (75 g) soft butter

6 oz (175 g) plain flour, sifted

1½ oz (40 g) Parmesan (Parmigiano Reggiano), finely grated

FOR THE FILLING:

1 oz (25 g) dried porcini mushrooms

3 oz (75 g) butter

2 small red onions, finely chopped

2 cloves garlic, chopped

6 oz (175 g) chestnut mushrooms

6 oz (175 g) open cap mushrooms

2 teaspoons lemon juice

1 heaped tablespoon chopped fresh parsley

6 x size 1 eggs

1 oz (25 g) Parmesan (Parmigiano Reggiano), finely grated, for sprinkling over the tarts

Sea salt and freshly milled black pepper

You will also need 6 quiche tins, 4-inch (10-cm) base diameter, ½ inch (1 cm) deep, and a 5½-inch (14-cm) plain cutter.

Begin by placing the porcini in a bowl. Pour 7 fl oz (200 ml) boiling water over them and leave to soak for 30 minutes.

Now make the pastry. This can easily be done in a processor or by rubbing the butter into the flour and stirring in the grated Parmesan and sufficient water (approximately 3 tablespoons) to mix to a soft but firm dough. Place the dough in a plastic bag and leave in the fridge for 30 minutes to rest. This pastry will need a little more water than usual as the cheese absorbs some of it.

For the filling, heat 2 oz (50 g) of the butter in a heavy-based frying pan, add the onions and garlic and fry until they are soft and almost transparent (about 15 minutes). While that's happening, finely chop the chestnut and open cap mushrooms. When the porcini have had their 30 minutes' soaking, place a sieve over a bowl and strain them into it, pressing to release the moisture. You can reserve the soaking liquid and freeze it for stocks or sauces if you don't want to throw it out.

Then chop the porcini finely and transfer them with the other mushrooms to the pan containing the onions. Add the remaining 1 oz (25 g) of butter, season and cook till the juices of the mushrooms run, then add the lemon juice and parsley. Raise the heat slightly and cook the mushrooms without a lid, stirring from time to time to prevent them sticking, until all the liquid has evaporated and the mixture is of a spreadable consistency. This will take about 25 minutes.

While the mushrooms are cooking, pre-heat the oven to gas mark 6, 400°F (200°C). Now roll out the pastry to a thickness of ⅛ inch (3 mm) and cut out 6 rounds, re-rolling the pastry if necessary.

Grease the tins with a little melted butter and line each tin with the pastry, pushing it down from the top so the pastry will not shrink while cooking. Trim any surplus pastry from around the top and prick the base with a fork. Now leave this in the fridge for a few minutes until the oven is up to temperature.

Now place the tins on a solid baking sheet and bake on the middle shelf of the oven for 15–20 minutes until the pastry is golden and crisp. Remove them from the oven and reduce the temperature to gas mark 4, 350°F (180°C).

Divide the filling between the tarts, making a well in the centre with the back of a spoon. Then break an egg into a saucer or a small ramekin, slip it into the tart and scatter a little Parmesan over the top. Repeat this process with the other five tarts and return them to the oven for 12–15 minutes until they are just set and the yolks are still soft and creamy. Serve straight away, because if they wait around the eggs will go on cooking.

◇

Spaghetti alla Carbonara

SERVES 2 AS A SUPPER DISH

This is my favourite, and the very best version I know of the great classic Italian recipe for pasta with bacon and egg sauce. This is one that is made using authentic ingredients: pancetta (Italian cured bacon which has a wonderful flavour) and Pecorino Romano (a sheep's cheese) which is sharper than Parmesan. However, if you can't get either of these ingredients it's still marvellous made with streaky bacon and Parmigiano Reggiano.

8 oz (225 g) spaghetti	**4 tablespoons crème fraîche**
2 x 70 g packs (or 5 oz) pancetta, sliced or ready cubed	**Salt and freshly milled black pepper**
1½ tablespoons extra virgin olive oil	TO SERVE:
4 tablespoons Pecorino Romano, finely grated	**Extra grated Pecorino**
2 x size 1 eggs plus 2 extra yolks	

First of all take your largest saucepan and fill it with at least 4 pints (2.25 litres) of hot water and then put it on the heat to come up to simmering point, adding salt and a few drops of olive oil. As soon as it reaches simmering point add the pasta and stir it once, then put a timer on and time it for 8 minutes exactly. (Some pasta might need 10 minutes so follow the instructions on the packet.)

Meanwhile, heat the olive oil in a frying pan and fry the pancetta until it's crisp and golden, about 5 minutes. Next, whisk the eggs, yolks, cheese and crème fraîche in a bowl and season generously with black pepper. Then when the pasta is cooked, drain it quickly in a colander, leaving a little of the moisture still clinging. Now quickly return it to the saucepan and add the pancetta and any oil in the pan, along with the egg and cream mixture. Stir very thoroughly so that everything gets a good coating – what happens is that the liquid egg cooks briefly as it comes into contact with the hot pasta.

Serve the pasta on really hot deep plates with some extra grated Pecorino.

Warm Lentil Salad with Walnuts and Goats' Cheese

SERVES 4

I think we should all be eating more pulses, so the more recipes that include them the better. In this warm salad, I've chosen the little tiny black-grey Puy lentils, but the green or brown variety will work just as well, given slightly less cooking time.

8 oz (225 g) Puy lentils	FOR THE DRESSING:
1½ oz (40 g) walnuts, roughly chopped	**1 fat clove garlic, peeled**
1 small red onion, finely chopped	**1 level teaspoon sea salt**
1 bay leaf	**1 rounded teaspoon powdered mustard**
1 fat clove garlic, crushed	**2 tablespoons balsamic vinegar**
1 heaped teaspoon thyme leaves, chopped	**2 tablespoons walnut oil**
1 tablespoon extra virgin olive oil	**3 tablespoons extra virgin olive oil**
Salt and freshly milled black pepper	**1 x 30 g pack (or 1 oz) of rocket leaves**
	Freshly milled black pepper
	2 crottin goats' cheese or 4 oz (110g) of any other firm goats' cheese

First you need to cook the lentils. To do this, heat the oil in a medium saucepan and when it's hot, lightly fry the chopped walnuts for about 1 minute. Then remove them with a draining spoon to a plate and keep them aside for later.

Now to the oil left in the pan, add the onion and crushed garlic and let these cook and soften for about 5 minutes. After that, stir in the lentils, bay leaf and thyme and make sure they all get a good coating with oil. Next add 10 fl oz (275 ml) of boiling water, but don't add any salt – just put a lid on, turn the heat down to a gentle simmer and let the lentils cook for 30–40 minutes or until they're tender and all the liquid has been absorbed. You really need to bite one to test if they're done.

While the lentils are cooking you can prepare the dressing. Use a pestle and mortar and crush the garlic with the salt until it's creamy, then add the mustard and work that into the garlic paste. After that, whisk in the balsamic vinegar, followed by the oils. Then season well with freshly milled black pepper.

As soon as the lentils are cooked, add salt to taste. Empty them into a warm serving bowl and while they're still hot, pour the dressing over. Give everything a good toss and stir, then crumble the goats' cheese all over and add the rocket leaves, torn in half. Give everything one more toss and stir, and serve straight away with the walnuts scattered over.

───────────── ◇ ─────────────

Baked Eggs in Wild Mushroom Tartlets (see page 30)

Blinis with Smoked Salmon, Crème Fraîche and Dill

SERVES 8 AS A STARTER

*B*linis originated in Russia and are traditionally made with buckwheat flour, but I find them better and lighter if made with a mixture of strong plain flour and buckwheat. Buckwheat is available in healthfood shops and some supermarkets, but if you can't get hold of it you can replace it with wholewheat flour. (See photograph on pages 36–7.)

2 oz (50 g) buckwheat flour	**1 teaspoon salt**
6 oz (175 g) strong white plain flour	**1½ oz (40 g) butter**
1 x 6 g sachet easy-blend dried yeast	
1 x 500 ml tub crème fraîche	FOR THE TOPPING:
(reserve 300 ml for the topping)	**1 lb (450 g) smoked salmon**
8 fl oz (225 ml) whole milk	**300 ml crème fraîche**
2 x size 1 eggs	**A few dill sprigs**

Begin by sifting the salt, buckwheat flour and plain flour together into a large roomy bowl and then sprinkle in the yeast. Place 7 fl oz (200 ml) of the crème fraîche into a measuring jug and add enough milk to bring it up to the 15 fl oz (425 ml) level. Place this in a small saucepan and warm it gently – it must only be slightly warm, as too much heat will kill the yeast. Next separate the eggs, reserving the whites until later, then add the yolks to the milk, mix them in with a whisk and after that pour the whole lot into the flour mixture. Whisk everything until you have a thick batter, then cover the bowl with a clean tea-cloth and leave it in a warm place for about 1 hour – this can simply be a matter of placing the bowl in another larger bowl filled with warm water.

After 1 hour the batter will be spongy and bubbly. Now you whisk up the egg whites until they form stiff peaks and gently fold them into the batter. Cover with the cloth again and leave as before for another hour.

When you're ready to make the blinis, begin by melting the butter in a heavy based frying pan, then tip the melted butter out into a cup and use it – with the help of a tightly rolled wodge of kitchen paper – to brush the pan all over as you make each blini. To do this keep the pan on a medium heat and add 1½ tablespoons of batter (1 tablespoon goes in first then another ½ tablespoon on top) – it won't spread out much and the underneath sets as soon as it touches the pan. This amount should give you a blini approximately 4 inches (10 cm) in diameter.

Don't worry at this stage if it looks too thick, it isn't, it's just light and puffy. After 40 seconds, no longer, flip the blini over and give it just 30 seconds on the other side. Transfer it to a wire cooling rack and repeat, brushing the pan with butter each time. This mixture should give you 24 blinis.

When all the blinis are made and have cooled, wrap them in foil parcels, with 6 laid out flat in each one. To serve, pre-heat the oven to gas mark 1, 275°F (140°C) and place the foil parcels on a high shelf for 10 minutes.

Serve the blinis on warm plates, giving each person 2 to start with, and top with slices of smoked salmon, about 2 oz (50 g) per person, add a tablespoon of very cold crème fraîche on the side of the plate and garnish with sprigs of fresh dill.

NOTE: Any unused blinis can be warmed and served for breakfast or tea with honey or jam. They also freeze very well if left in the foil parcels and can be re-heated in the oven, as above, after defrosting. If you want to serve blini canapés, these are made in the same way with teaspoonfuls of the mixture. Cook them for about 15 seconds on each side. Then re-heat, as above, and top with smoked salmon, crème fraîche and dill.

———————————◇———————————

Next page: Blinis with Smoked Salmon,
Crème Fraîche and Dill

Camembert Croquettes with Fresh Date and Apple Chutney

SERVES 6 AS A STARTER

Ripe Camembert is essential for this recipe, so plan ahead and buy a Camembert which will be ready to use roughly on its sell-by date. I keep mine in the garage or in the boot of a car, which is cool enough in the winter, though you have to warn people about the smell!

1 x 250 g (9 oz) round, ripe unpasteurized Normandy Camembert, chilled
1 small carrot
½ small onion
½ stick celery
10 fl oz (275 ml) whole milk
1 pinch or blade of mace
1 bay leaf
6 peppercorns
1½ oz (40 g) butter
2 oz (50 g) plain flour
Groundnut oil for frying

FOR THE COATING:

2 x size 1 eggs
2 tablespoons milk
6 oz (175 g) fine white breadcrumbs
1 tablespoon seasoned flour

TO SERVE:

6 flat-leaf parsley sprigs

You will also need 6 x 4-fl oz (110-ml) straight-sided ramekins 2¾ inches (7 cm) diameter and some clingfilm.

First of all peel and roughly chop the vegetables and place them in a saucepan with the milk, mace, bay leaf and peppercorns. Bring everything up to simmering point, then turn the heat off and leave to infuse for 30 minutes.

After that strain the milk into a jug, using a sieve and pressing the vegetables with the back of a spoon to extract all the juices. Now rinse and dry the saucepan and, over a medium heat, melt the butter in it, then add the flour and, using a wooden spoon, stir briskly until the mixture has turned a pale straw colour.

Now add the milk a little at a time and switch to a balloon whisk, whisking vigorously after each addition until you have a very thick, glossy mixture. Then take the pan off the heat and allow it to cool slightly.

While the mixture is cooling you can deal with the cheese – although it needs to be ripe, it makes life a lot easier if it has been chilled. So all you do is cut the Camembert in half and, using a small sharp knife, peel it carefully, paring the skin away from the cheese. After that, add the cheese to the sauce in smallish pieces and give it all a really good mixing to combine it as thoroughly as possible. Then leave it aside for 10 minutes or so to cool.

Meanwhile, prepare the ramekins. The easiest way to do this is to lightly oil each one, then take pieces of clingfilm about 8 inches (20 cm) long and lay them across the centre of each ramekin. Then, using a clean pastry brush, push the clingfilm into the ramekins all round the edges – it doesn't matter if it creases. Now divide the cheese mixture between each one and press it in evenly. Fold the surplus clingfilm over the top, smooth it out, then place them in the fridge for several hours, but preferably overnight.

The croquettes can be coated with the egg and breadcumbs in advance, provided that you keep them well chilled afterwards. Sprinkle the seasoned flour onto a piece of greaseproof paper, then lightly beat the eggs and milk together and spread the breadcrumbs out on a plate. Also, have another flat plate to hand.

Now all you do is unfold the clingfilm and flip each croquette onto the flour and lightly coat it on all sides. Next dip it in the beaten egg, then in the breadcrumbs, shaking off any surplus. Now return it to the egg and then back again to the breadcrumbs. This double coating gives good protection while the croquettes are cooking.

When the croquettes are coated, if you're not cooking them straight away, put them on the flat plate and return them to the fridge, uncovered. When you're ready to cook them, have some crumpled kitchen paper spread out on a plate and then heat up enough groundnut oil to just cover the base of a solid frying pan. The oil needs to be really hot, so test it by dropping in a little cube of bread and if it turns golden in 30 seconds the oil is ready. Now fry the croquettes for about 2 minutes on each side and transfer them to kitchen paper to drain while you fry the rest. You need to take some care here not to overcook them – it's okay for little bits to ooze out of the sides, but if you leave them in too long they tend to collapse. Serve as soon as possible after they are cooked. Garnish with sprigs of parsley and the chutney alongside.

———————— ◇ ————————

Fresh Date and Apple Chutney

3 oz (75 g) fresh stoned dates	2 whole cloves
(or dried if not available)	3 tablespoons balsamic vinegar
2 small Granny Smith apples	2 shallots, peeled and roughly chopped
⅓ teaspoon allspice berries	Pinch cayenne pepper

This chutney is best made a couple of hours in advance. First, using a pestle and mortar, crush the spices to a fine powder. Quarter and core the apples, but leave the peel on, then cut each quarter into 8.

Place the apples, dates and all the rest of the ingredients in a food processor, give it all a good whizz to start, then use the pulse action to chop everything evenly. Then transfer the whole lot into a serving bowl, cover with clingfilm and chill before serving.

———————— ◇ ————————

Apple, Cider Salad with Melted Camembert Dressing

SERVES 6 AS A STARTER OR 2 AS A LIGHT LUNCH

*W*hen I wrote the 'Summer Collection' I felt I'd got Caesar salad as perfect as it could be, but then I ate so many Caesar salads that I began to get bored. If this has happened to you too, then let me tell you that this makes an absolutely brilliant alternative, especially in the winter months. It does need ripe Camembert, but if you don't live near a supplier, a supermarket Camembert will have a date stamp to show when it will have fully ripened, so you can gauge the best time to make the salad (see previous recipe). The piquancy of the apple combined with cheese is absolutely superb.

FOR THE SALAD:

1 Cos lettuce

4 oz (110 g) Cox's apple (1 medium)

1 x 30 g pack (or 1 oz) rocket leaves

FOR THE DRESSING:

1 x 250 g (9 oz) round, ripe unpasteurized Normandy Camembert, chilled

2 rounded tablespoons crème fraîche

1 or 2 tablespoons dry cider (if Camembert isn't quite ripe)

TO SERVE:

1 quantity of garlic croûtons (see page 10)

First make the garlic croûtons (see page 10). Then prepare the dressing – cut the cheese in half and use a small, sharp knife to peel it carefully like a potato, paring away the skin from the soft cheese. Place the cheese in a small saucepan. Next measure in the crème fraîche but don't heat it until just before you are going to serve the salad.

When you're ready, mix the salad leaves together, breaking up the larger ones into manageable pieces, and arrange the salad on the serving plates. Slice the apple, leaving the skin on, and put the slices in a small bowl, then sprinkle on a little cider – just enough to give the slices a covering. After that, pat them dry and arrange over the salad leaves.

Now place the saucepan over a gentle heat and blend the cheese and crème fraîche together for about 3–4 minutes – using a small balloon whisk – until the mixture is smooth. If the cheese is very ripe and runny, you may not need the dry cider, but if the centre is less ripe, you will need to add a little cider to keep the mixture smooth. The main thing is to melt the cheese just sufficiently for it to run off the whisk in ribbons, while still retaining its texture. Don't allow the cheese to overheat or it may go stringy – it needs to be melted rather than cooked.

Next, using a small ladle, pour the dressing equally over the salad and finish with a scattering of croûtons. Alternatively, you can hand the dressing round the table and let everyone help themselves.

NOTE: You can, if you want to, prepare the dressing ahead, then just gently melt it again before serving.

Apple, Cider Salad with Melted Camembert Dressing

Home-made Mayonnaise

Home-made mayonnaise made by the traditional method is unbeatable. First a couple of tips: (a) use a small basin with a narrow base – a 1-pint (570-ml) pudding basin is ideal, and (b) place the basin on a damp tea towel so it will remain steady and leave you two hands free, one to drip the oil, the other to hold the beater.

10 fl oz (275 ml) groundnut oil	**1 level teaspoon salt**
2 x size 1 egg yolks	**Freshly milled black pepper**
1 clove garlic, crushed	**1 teaspoon white wine vinegar**
1 heaped teaspoon powdered mustard	

First of all put the egg yolks into the basin, add the crushed garlic, mustard powder, salt and a little freshly milled black pepper. Mix all of these together well. Then, holding the groundnut oil in a jug in one hand and an electric hand whisk in the other, add 1 drop of oil to the egg mixture and whisk this in.

However stupid it may sound, the key to a successful mayonnaise is making sure each drop of oil is thoroughly whisked in before adding the next drop. It won't take all day, because after a few minutes – once you've added several drops of oil – the mixture will begin to thicken and go very stiff and lumpy. When it gets to this stage you need to add a teaspoon of vinegar, which will thin the mixture down.

Now the critical point has passed so you can then begin pouring the oil in a very, very thin but steady stream, keeping the beaters going all the time. When all the oil has been added, taste and add more salt and pepper if it needs it. If you'd like the mayonnaise to be a bit lighter, at this stage add 2 tablespoons of boiling water and whisk it in.

Mayonnaise only curdles when you add the oil too quickly at the beginning. If that happens, don't despair. All you need to do is put a fresh egg yolk into a clean basin, add the curdled mixture to it (drop by drop), then continue adding the rest of the oil as though nothing had happened.

The mayonnaise should be stored in a screw-top jar in the bottom of the fridge, but for no longer than a week.

———————————— ◇ ————————————

Home-made Mayonnaise

Prawn Cocktail 2000

SERVES 6

*T*his recipe is part of my sixties revival menu. In those days it used to be something simple but really luscious, yet over the years it has suffered from some very poor adaptations, not least watery prawns and inferior sauces. So here, in all its former glory, is a starter quite definitely fit for the new millennium!

2 lb (900 g) large prawns in their shells (see recipe)	FOR THE SAUCE:
	1 quantity of mayonnaise (see page 45)
1 crisp-hearted lettuce, such as Cos	**1 dessertspoon Worcestershire sauce**
1 x 30 g pack (or 1 oz) rocket leaves	**A few drops Tabasco sauce**
1 ripe but firm avocado pear	**1 dessertspoon lime juice**
1 whole lime, divided into 6 wedge-shaped sections	**2 tablespoons tomato ketchup (preferably organic)**
Cayenne pepper	**Salt and freshly milled black pepper**

The very best version of this is made with prawns (either fresh or frozen in their shells) that you have cooked yourself. Failing that, buy the large cooked prawns in their shells, or if you can only get shelled prawns cut the amount to 1 lb (450 g). To prepare them: if frozen put them in a colander and allow to defrost thoroughly at room temperature for about 1 hour. After that heat a large solid frying pan or wok and dry-fry the prawns for 4–5 minutes until the grey turns a vibrant pink. As soon as they're cool, reserve 6 in their shells for a garnish and peel the remainder. Then take a small sharp knife, make a cut along the back of each peeled prawn and remove any black thread. Place them in a bowl, cover with clingfilm and keep in the fridge until needed.

To make the cocktail sauce, prepare the mayonnaise (see page 45) and add it to the rest of the sauce ingredients. Stir and taste to check the seasoning, then keep the sauce covered with clingfilm in the fridge until needed.

When you are ready to serve, shred the lettuce and rocket fairly finely and divide them between 6 stemmed glasses, then peel and chop the avocado into small dice and scatter this in each glass amongst the lettuce. Top with the prawns and the sauce, sprinkle a dusting of cayenne pepper on top and garnish with 1 section of lime and 1 unpeeled prawn per glass. Serve with brown bread and butter.

◇

Warm Poached Egg Salad with Frizzled Chorizo

SERVES 4

This makes a fun starter for four people, or a zappy light lunch or supper dish for two. For poaching you need very fresh eggs, so watch the date stamp on the box when you buy them and, to be absolutely sure, pop them into a glass measuring jug filled with cold water: if the eggs sit horizontally on the base they're very fresh. A slight tilt is acceptable, but if they sit vertically your supplier's date stamps are in doubt.

Chorizo is a spicy Spanish pork sausage made with paprika. At specialist food shops you can also buy 'chorizo piccante', a more spicy version, which gives the whole thing a wonderful kick.

4 x very fresh size 1 eggs	**1½ tablespoons sherry vinegar**
6 oz (175 g) chorizo sausage, skinned and cut into ¼-inch (5-mm) cubes	**Salt and freshly milled black pepper**
	3 oz (75 g) assorted green salad leaves
3 tablespoons extra virgin olive oil	
1 medium onion, finely chopped	TO SERVE:
2 cloves garlic, finely chopped	**1 quantity of croûtons (see page 10)**
1 red pepper, de-seeded and chopped small	**with the addition of 1 level tablespoon hot paprika**
3 tablespoons dry sherry	

First make the croûtons by following the basic recipe on page 10 but sprinkle the paprika over the bread cubes before the olive oil.

When you're ready to make the salad, start with the eggs. A useful way to poach 4 eggs without any last-minute hassle is to pour boiling water straight from the kettle into a medium-sized frying pan. Place it over a heat gentle enough for there to be the merest trace of bubbles simmering on the base of the pan. Now carefully break the 4 eggs into the water and let them cook for just 1 minute. Then remove the pan from the heat and leave the eggs in the hot water for 10 minutes, after which time the whites will be set and the yolks creamy.

Now arrange the salad leaves on 4 plates. Then, in another frying pan, heat 1 tablespoon of the olive oil until it's very hot, then add the chorizo, cook for 2–3 minutes then add the onion, garlic and pepper. Keeping them on the move and turning down the heat if it gets too hot, cook for about 6 minutes until the ingredients are toasted round the edge. Now add the sherry, sherry vinegar and the remaining 2 tablespoons of olive oil to the pan. Let it all bubble a bit and season with salt and pepper.

To remove the eggs from the first pan, use a draining spoon with a wad of kitchen paper underneath to absorb the moisture. Place them centrally on the salad leaves on the serving plates, pour the warm chorizo dressing over everything, and finally sprinkle on the croûtons. We eat this with olive bread to mop up the juices – a wonderful accompaniment.

NOTE: If you like you can make this with red wine and red wine vinegar or white wine and white wine vinegar just to ring the changes.

CHAPTER THREE

SEAFOOD *in* WINTER

◇

I wouldn't be at all surprised if fish became *the* food for the 21st century. Fish has just about everything going for it: what other food can you think of that provides first-class protein, is low in fat and calories yet at the same time cooks faster than almost anything else? While I was researching and preparing this chapter, I actually made a personal vow to include much more fish in my daily cooking routine, not least because it's so quick. You can provide such a great variety of interesting and up-to-the-minute supper dishes in as little as 10 minutes – and very few fish dishes take longer than half an hour.

One of the reasons it all got so much easier is that although, sadly, the high street fishmonger is an endangered species, fish in supermarkets has taken on a whole new dimension in that it has become far more accessible and a great deal of the tedious work once involved in its preparation has been removed. Fish nowadays comes cleaned and gutted, boned and filleted and sometimes even skinned. Also with supplies now coming in from all corners of the world and at all times of the year, there is a far wider choice than ever. So for a more varied and interesting diet without too much work, let's all of us vow to eat more fish!

Fillets of Sole Véronique

SERVES 2 AS MAIN COURSE OR 4 AS A STARTER

*T*his famous French classic has always been a favourite of mine and, as it has somehow been neglected on restaurant menus, I think it's time for a revival. Personally I love to serve it with the grapes well chilled, which beautifully complements the warm rich sauce. However, if you prefer you could add the grapes to the fish before it goes under the grill, so they would be warmed through.

2 good-sized Dover or lemon sole about 12–16 oz (350–450 g). Ask your fishmonger to fillet and skin them for you	**½ oz (10 g) butter**
	½ oz (10 g) plain flour
3 oz (75 g) Muscat-type grapes	**5 fl oz (150 ml) whipping cream**
1 heaped teaspoon chopped fresh tarragon	**Salt and freshly milled black pepper**
6 fl oz (175 ml) Chambéry vermouth or dry white wine	

You will also need an ovenproof serving dish.

First peel the grapes well in advance by placing them in a bowl and pouring boiling water over them. Leave them for 45 seconds, then drain off the water and you will find the skins will slip off easily. Cut the grapes in half, remove the seeds, then return them to the bowl and cover and chill in the refrigerator until needed.

When you are ready to start cooking the fish, begin by warming the serving dish and have a sheet of foil ready. Then wipe each sole fillet and divide each one in half lengthways by cutting along the natural line, so you now have 8 fillets. Season them and roll each one up as tightly as possible, keeping the skin side on the inside and starting the roll at the narrow end. Next put a faint smear of butter on the base of a medium frying pan and arrange the sole fillets in it. Then sprinkle in the tarragon followed by the vermouth.

Now place the pan on a medium heat and bring it up to simmering point. Cover, then put a timer on and poach the fillets for 3–4 minutes, depending on their thickness. While the fish is poaching pre-heat the grill to its highest setting.

Meanwhile take a small saucepan, melt the butter in it, stir in the flour to make a smooth paste and let it cook gently, stirring all the time, until it has become a pale straw colour. When the fish is cooked transfer the fillets with a fish slice to the warmed dish, cover with foil and keep warm.

Next boil the fish-poaching liquid in its pan until it has reduced to about a third of its original volume. Stir in the cream and let that come up to a gentle simmer, then gradually add this cream and liquid mixture to the flour and butter mixture in the small saucepan, whisking it in well until you have a thin, creamy sauce. Taste and season with salt and freshly milled black pepper.

Pour the sauce over the fish and pop it under the pre-heated grill (about 4 inches from the source of the heat) and leave it there for approximately 3 minutes, until it is glazed golden brown on top. Serve each portion on to warmed serving plates, garnished with grapes.

Luxury Fish Pie with Rösti Caper Topping

SERVES 4–6

This is a perfect recipe for entertaining and wouldn't need anything to go with it other than a simple green salad. The fish can be varied according to what's available as long as you have 2¼ lb (1 kg) in total.

FOR THE FISH MIXTURE:	
1½ lb (700 g) halibut	

1 dessertspoon chopped fresh dill

Salt and freshly milled black pepper

FOR THE FISH MIXTURE:
1½ lb (700 g) halibut
8 oz (225 g) king scallops, including the coral, cut in half
4 oz (110 g) uncooked tiger prawns, throughly defrosted if frozen, and peeled
5 fl oz (150 ml) dry white wine
10 fl oz (275 ml) carton of fish stock
1 bay leaf
2 oz (50 g) butter
2 oz (50 g) plain flour
2 tablespoons crème fraîche
6 cornichons (continental gherkins), drained, rinsed and chopped
1 heaped tablespoon chopped fresh parsley

FOR THE ROSTI CAPER TOPPING:
2 lb (900 g) Désirée or Romano potatoes, even-sized if possible
1 tablespoon salted capers or capers in brine, drained, rinsed and dried
2 oz (50 g) butter, melted
2 oz (50 g) strong Cheddar cheese, finely grated

You will also need a baking dish about 2 inches (5 cm) deep of 2½-pint (1.5-litre) capacity, well-buttered.

Pre-heat the oven to gas mark 7, 425°F (220°C).

First of all, prepare the potatoes by scrubbing them, but leaving the skins on. As they all have to cook at the same time, if there are any larger ones cut them in half. Then place them in a saucepan with enough boiling, salted water to barely cover them and cook them for 12 minutes after they have come back to the boil, covered with the lid. Strain off the water and cover them with a clean tea-cloth to absorb the steam.

Meanwhile, heat the wine and stock in a medium saucepan, add the bay leaf and some seasoning, then cut the fish in half if it's a large piece, add it to the saucepan and poach the fish gently for 5 minutes. It should be slightly undercooked.

Then remove the fish to a plate, using a draining spoon, and strain the liquid through a sieve into a bowl.

Now rinse the pan you cooked the fish in, melt the butter in it, whisk in the flour and gently cook for 2 minutes. Then gradually add the strained fish stock little by little, whisking all the time. When you have a smooth sauce turn the heat to its lowest setting and let the sauce gently cook for 5 minutes. Then whisk in the crème fraîche, followed by the cornichons, parsley and dill. Give it all a good seasoning and remove it from the heat.

To make the rösti, peel the potatoes and, using the coarse side of a grater, grate them into long shreds into a bowl. Then add the capers and the melted butter and, using two forks, lightly toss everything together so that the potatoes get a good coating of butter.

SEAFOOD *IN* WINTER

Now remove the skin from the white fish and divide it into chunks, quite large if possible, and combine the fish with the sauce. Next, if you're going to cook the fish pie more or less immediately, all you do is add the raw scallops and prawns to the fish mixture then spoon it into a well-buttered baking dish. Sprinkle the rösti on top, spreading it out as evenly as possible and not pressing it down too firmly. Then finally scatter the cheese over the surface and bake on a high shelf of the oven for 35–40 minutes.

If you want to make the fish pie in advance, this is possible as long as you remember to let the sauce get completely cold before adding the cooled white fish and raw scallops and prawns. When the topping is on, cover the dish loosely with clingfilm and refrigerate it until you're ready to cook it. Then give it an extra 5–10 minutes' cooking time.

Fried Herring Fillets with a Lime Pepper Crust

SERVES 2

For me the humble herring, once the food of the poor, is a great delicacy with all the gutsy flavours of fresh sardines but lots more juicy flesh. Now they can be bought boned and filleted and are cooked in moments. This recipe is probably the fastest in this chapter. The lime and pepper crust is fragrant and slightly crunchy. Squeeze lots of lime juice over before you start eating – it cuts through the richness perfectly.

2 herring fillets weighing 6–7 oz (175–200 g) each	Grated zest and juice of 2 limes
1 rounded teaspoon whole mixed peppercorns	1 rounded dessertspoon plain flour
	2 tablespoons olive oil
	Crushed salt flakes

First of all crush the peppercorns with a pestle and mortar – not too fine, so they still have some texture. Then grate the zest of the limes and add half of it to the peppercorns, then add the flour. Mix them all together and spread the mixture out on a flat plate. Wipe the herrings dry with kitchen paper and coat the flesh side with the flour-pepper mixture. Press the fish well in to give it a good coating – anything left on the plate can be used to dust the skin side lightly.

Now in your largest frying pan, heat the oil until it is very hot and fry the herrings flesh-side down for about 2–3 minutes. Have a peek by lifting up the edge with a fish slice – it should be golden. Then turn the fish over on to the other side and give it another 2 minutes, and drain on crumpled greaseproof or kitchen paper before serving. Serve sprinkled with crushed salt, the rest of the lime zest and the limes cut into quarters to squeeze over.

Smoked Haddock with Spinach and Chive Butter Sauce

SERVES 4

My thanks to top chef and dear friend Simon Hopkinson for this superb recipe which he cooked for me at his restaurant Bibendum one day for lunch – and had invented that day! Now, thanks to his generosity, all of us can make and savour what has become one of my very favourite fish recipes.

4 pieces smoked haddock, approximately 6 oz (175 g) each, skinned and boned	3 x size 1 egg yolks
	2 tablespoons chopped chives
10 fl oz (275 ml) milk	Salt and freshly milled black pepper
Freshly milled black pepper	
	FOR THE SPINACH:
	2 lb (900 g) raw spinach, picked over, trimmed and thoroughly washed
FOR THE HOLLANDAISE SAUCE:	
6 oz (175 g) butter, melted	1 oz (25 g) butter
1 tablespoon lemon juice	Salt and freshly milled black pepper

First you need to make the Hollandaise sauce: place the butter in a small saucepan and let it melt slowly. Meanwhile blend the egg yolks and seasoning in a liquidizer or food processor.

Then turn the heat up and when the butter reaches the boil, pour it into a jug and start to pour this very slowly into the liquidizer, in a thin trickle, with the motor running, until all the butter is added and the sauce is thickened. Then, with the motor still switched on, slowly add the lemon juice. Then keep the sauce warm by placing it in a basin over some hot water.

To cook the fish, place it in a frying pan, pour in the milk, add some freshly milled pepper then bring it all up to a gentle simmer. Cover and poach for 6–7 minutes. While that is happening, cook the spinach – melt the butter in a large saucepan and pile the spinach in with a teaspoon of salt and some freshly milled black pepper. Put the lid on and cook it over a medium heat for 2–3 minutes, turning it all over halfway through. Quite a bit of water will come out so what you need to do then is drain it in a colander and press down a small plate on top to squeeze out every last bit of juice. Cover with a cloth and keep warm.

When the haddock is ready divide the spinach between 4 warm serving plates, and place the haddock pieces on top. Now just add a little of the poaching liquid (about 2 tablespoons) to the sauce and whisk it in along with the chives then pour the sauce over the haddock and spinach, and serve straight away.

———————◇———————

Smoked Haddock with Spinach and Chive Butter Sauce

Seared Spiced Salmon Steaks with Black Bean Salsa

SERVES 6

Everyone I know who has eaten this has loved it. The black bean salsa looks very pretty along-side the salmon and provides a marvellous contrast of flavours and textures, and what's more the whole thing is so little trouble to prepare.

	FOR THE SALSA:
6 salmon steaks, 5–6 oz (150–175 g) each	4 oz (110 g) black beans soaked overnight in twice their volume of cold water
3 fat cloves garlic	
2 level teaspoons rock salt	
1½-inch (4-cm) piece of root ginger	12 oz (350 g) ripe but firm tomatoes, skinned, de-seeded and finely chopped
Grated zest of 2 limes, reserve the juice for the salsa	1 red chilli, de-seeded and finely chopped
A good pinch of ground cinnamon	
A good pinch of ground cumin	
1 x 15 g pack (or ½ oz) fresh coriander leaves (reserve 6 sprigs and finely chop the remainder)	1 x 15 g pack (or ½ oz) coriander leaves, finely chopped
	1 medium red onion, finely chopped
2 tablespoons light olive oil	1 tablespoon extra virgin olive oil
Freshly milled black pepper	Juice of the limes reserved from the salmon recipe
	½ level teaspoon salt

You will also need a solid baking sheet that won't buckle under the heat.

A few hours before you want to cook the salmon, wipe each of the steaks with damp kitchen paper and remove any visible bones using tweezers. Place the salmon on a plate, then, with a pestle and mortar, crush the garlic cloves and rock salt together until you have a creamy purée. Now add the grated ginger, lime zest, cinnamon and cumin, 1 tablespoon of olive oil and the chopped coriander, and a good grind of black pepper. Mix everything together and spread a little of this mixture on each salmon steak. Cover with clingfilm and set aside for the flavours to develop and permeate the salmon.

To make the salsa, rinse the beans in plenty of cold water, put them in a saucepan with enough water to cover, bring to the boil and boil rapidly for 10 minutes. Then reduce the heat and simmer the beans for 30 minutes until tender. Drain and allow them to cool completely before adding all the other ingredients. Then leave them covered for several hours to allow the flavours to develop.

When you're ready to cook the salmon, pre-heat the grill to its highest setting. Brush the baking sheet with the olive oil and put it under the grill to heat up. When the grill is really hot, remove the baking sheet using an oven glove, and place the salmon pieces on it. They will sear and sizzle as they touch the hot metal. Position the tray 3 inches (7.5 cm) from the heat and grill them for 7 minutes exactly. Use a kitchen timer as the timing is vital.

Remove them when the time is up and use a sharp knife to ease the skins off. Transfer to warm plates and garnish with sprigs of coriander. Serve immediately with the black bean salsa.

Salmon Coulibiac

SERVES 6

This is one of the best fish pies ever invented. It's perfect for entertaining as it can all be made well in advance and popped into the oven just before you serve the first course. Serve it cut in slices, with a large bowl of mixed leaf salad tossed in a sharp lemony dressing and hand round some foaming Hollandaise sauce. Or you can simply melt some butter with an equal quantity of lemon juice and serve it with that.

1 x 375g pack of ready-rolled fresh puff pastry	**1½ tablespoons chopped fresh parsley**
1¼ lb (560 g) salmon tail fillet, skinned	**Salt and freshly milled black pepper**
3 oz (75 g) butter	
3 oz (75 g) white basmati rice	TO FINISH:
8 fl oz (225 ml) fish stock	**1 egg, lightly beaten**
1 medium onion, finely chopped	**1 oz (25 g) butter, melted**
4 oz (110 g) small button mushrooms, finely sliced	
1 tablespoon freshly chopped dill	
1 teaspoon lemon zest	You will also need a good solid baking tray
2 tablespoons fresh lemon juice	16 x 12 inches (40 x 30 cm) and a lattice cutter.
2 x size 1 eggs, hard boiled (7 minutes from simmering), roughly chopped	Pre-heat the oven to gas mark 4, 350°F (180°C).

First melt 1 oz (25 g) of the butter in a medium saucepan and stir in the rice. When the rice is coated with butter, add the stock and a little salt and bring it up to simmering point, then stir well and cover with a lid. Cook the rice for 15 minutes exactly, then take the pan off the heat, remove the lid and allow it to cool.

As soon as the rice is cooking, take a sheet of buttered foil, lay the salmon on it and add some seasoning. Then wrap it up loosely, pleating the foil at the top and folding the edges in. Place it on a baking sheet and pop it in the oven for just 10 minutes – the salmon needs to be only half cooked. After that remove it from the oven, open the foil and allow it to cool.

While the salmon and the rice are cooling, melt the other 2 oz (50 g) of butter in a small saucepan and gently sweat the onion in it for about 10 minutes until it softens. After that add the sliced mushrooms and half the dill, then carry on cooking gently for a further 5 minutes. After that stir in the lemon zest and juice, some salt and freshly milled black pepper, and allow this mixture to cool.

Next take a large bowl and combine the salmon, broken up into large flakes, the hard-boiled eggs, the remaining dill and half the parsley. Give all this a good seasoning of salt and freshly milled black pepper. Next, in another bowl, combine the rice mixture with onion, mushroom and the rest of the parsley, giving this some seasoning too.

Now for the pastry. What you need to do here is take it out of its packet, unfold it and place it lengthways on a lightly floured surface, then using a tape measure, roll the pastry into a 14-inch (35-cm) square. Now cut it into 2 lengths, one 6½ inches (16 cm) and one 7½ inches (19 cm). Lightly brush the baking sheet and surface of the pastry with melted butter and lay the narrower strip of pastry onto it. Then first spoon half the rice mixture along the centre leaving a gap of at least 1 inch (2.5 cm) all the way round. Next spoon the salmon mixture on top of the rice, building it up as high as possible and pressing and moulding it with your hands – what you're aiming for is a loaf shape of mixture. Then lightly mould the rest of the rice mixture on top of the salmon and brush the 1-inch (2.5-cm) border all round with beaten egg.

Next take the lattice cutter and run it along the centre of the other piece of pastry leaving an even margin of about 1 inch (2.5 cm) all round. Brush the surface of the pastry with the remaining melted butter, then very carefully lift this and cover the salmon mixture with it. The idea here is not to let the lattice open too much as you lift it, because it will open naturally as it goes over the filling. Press the edges together all round to seal, then trim the pastry so that you're left with a ¾-inch (2-cm) border. Now using the back edge of a knife, knock up the edges of the pastry, then crimp it all along using your thumb and the back of the knife, pulling the knife towards the filling each time as you go round. Alternatively just fork it all around.

When you're ready to cook the coulibiac raise the oven temperature to gas mark 7, 425°F (220°C) and brush the surface of the pastry all over with beaten egg and any remaining butter. And, if you feel like it, you can re-roll some of the trimmings and cut out little fish shapes to decorate the top. Now place the coulibiac onto the high shelf of the oven and bake it for 20–25 minutes until it's golden brown. Remove it from the oven and leave it to rest for about 10 minutes before cutting into slices and serving with the sauce.

NOTE: Provided everything is cooled thoroughly first you can make the coulibiac in advance. Cover it with clingfilm and leave in the fridge until you want to cook it.

————————◇————————

Foaming Hollandaise

2 x size 1 eggs, separated	**4 oz (110 g) salted butter**
1 dessertspoon white wine vinegar	**Salt and freshly milled black pepper**
1 dessertspoon lemon juice	

To make the foaming Hollandaise sauce, begin by placing the egg yolks in a food processor or blender together with some salt, switch on and blend them thoroughly. In a small saucepan heat the vinegar and lemon juice till the mixture simmers, then switch the processor on again and pour the hot liquid onto the egg yolks in a steady stream. Switch off.

Now in the same saucepan melt the butter – not too fiercely: it mustn't brown. When it is liquid and foaming, switch on the processor once more and pour in the butter, again in a steady thin stream, until it is all incorporated and the sauce has thickened. Next, in a small bowl, whisk the egg whites until they form soft peaks and then fold the sauce, a tablespoon at a time, into the egg whites and taste to check the seasoning. When you've done that it's ready to serve or it can be left till later and placed in a bowl over barely simmering water to gently warm through.

Foil-Baked Salmon served with English Parsley Sauce

SERVES 4

Now that farmed salmon is plentiful and available all the year round, we can all enjoy luxury fish at affordable prices. However, this recipe works equally well using cod cutlets, halibut or other firm white fish. Another luxury – perhaps because of its sheer rarity nowadays – is a classic parsley sauce, so simple but so delightfully good.

4 salmon steaks weighing approximately 6 oz (175 g) each	**1 blade mace**
A few parsley stalks	**A few chopped parsley stalks**
4 small bay leaves	**10 whole black peppercorns**
4 slices lemon	**¾ oz (20 g) plain flour**
4 dessertspoons dry white wine	**1½ oz (40 g) butter**
Salt and freshly milled black pepper	**4 heaped tablespoons finely chopped parsley**
FOR THE PARSLEY SAUCE:	**1 tablespoon single cream**
15 fl oz (425 ml) milk	**1 teaspoon lemon juice**
1 bay leaf	**Salt and freshly milled black pepper**
1 slice of onion, ¼ inch (5 mm) thick	

You will also need a solid baking sheet.

To make the sauce, place the milk, bay leaf, onion slice, mace, peppercorns and a few chopped parsley stalks in a saucepan. Bring slowly up to simmering point, pour the mixture into a bowl and leave it aside to get completely cold. Meanwhile, to prepare the salmon, take a sheet of foil large enough to wrap all the fish steaks in, and lay it over a shallow baking tray. Wipe the pieces of salmon with kitchen paper and place on the foil. Then place the parsley stalks, a bay leaf and a slice of lemon over each steak, and season with salt and pepper. Finally, sprinkle the wine over, bring the foil up either side, then pleat it, fold it over and seal it at the ends.

When you need to cook the salmon, pre-heat the oven to gas mark 4, 350°F (180°C) and bake the salmon on a highish oven shelf for 20 minutes exactly. Then, before serving, slip off the skin, using a sharp knife to make a cut and just pulling it off all round.

When you're ready to make the sauce, strain the milk back into the saucepan, discarding the flavourings, then add the flour and butter and bring everything gradually up to simmering point, whisking continuously with a balloon whisk until the sauce has thickened. Now turn the heat down to its lowest possible setting and let the sauce cook for 5 minutes, stirring from time to time. When you're ready to serve the sauce, add the parsley, cream and lemon juice. Taste and add seasoning, then transfer to a warm jug to pour over the fish at the table.

Gratin of Mussels with Melted Camembert

SERVES 6 AS A STARTER

I *first sampled this concept in Normandy where the Camembert was used as a topping for oysters. Then back home, I discovered it goes superbly well with mussels too.*

2 lb (900 g) mussels, cleaned and prepared

1 tablespoon olive oil

1 shallot, chopped

1 clove garlic

6 fl oz (175 ml) dry white wine

Salt and freshly milled black pepper

FOR THE TOPPING:

1 x 250 g (9 oz) slightly under-ripe Normandy Camembert, de-rinded and cut into small cubes

2 oz (50 g) fresh breadcrumbs

2 tablespoons finely chopped fresh parsley

2 cloves garlic, finely chopped

Salt and freshly milled black pepper

TO SERVE:

Crusty bread

You will also need a baking tray measuring 12 x 16 inches (30 x 40 cm).

First you need to deal with the mussels: heat the olive oil in a large pan, add the shallot and garlic and cook these over a medium heat for about 5 minutes or until they're just soft. Now turn the heat up high, tip in the prepared mussels and add the wine and some salt and pepper. Put on a close-fitting lid, turn the heat down to medium and cook the mussels for about 5 minutes, shaking the pan once or twice, or until they have all opened. Discard any that remain closed. When the mussels are cooked pull away the top shells and discard them. Arrange the mussels sitting on their half shells on a baking tray. Then put ½ teaspoon of strained mussel juice into each shell.

Now place a cube of Camembert on top of each mussel. Then, in a bowl, combine the breadcrumbs, parsley, garlic and a seasoning of salt and pepper and sprinkle this mixture on top.

When you are ready to finish the mussels, pre-heat the grill to its highest setting for at least 10 minutes, then place the tray of mussels fairly close to the heat source and don't go away. You need to watch them like a hawk. It will only take about 3–4 minutes for the cheese to melt and turn golden brown and bubbling. Serve straight away with lots of crusty bread.

◇

Linguine with Mussels and Walnut Parsley Pesto

SERVES 2

For me, mussels are still a luxury food that cost very little money. I don't think anything can match their exquisite, fresh-from-the-sea flavour. In this recipe every precious drop of mussel juice is used which gives a lovely, concentrated flavour. Now that mussels come ready cleaned and prepared, it makes the whole thing very simple and easy: all you have to do is put them in cold water, then pull off any beardy strands with a sharp knife, use them as soon as possible and discard any that don't close tightly when given a sharp tap.

2 lb (900 g) mussels, cleaned and prepared	FOR THE PESTO:
	½ oz (10 g) walnuts, chopped
6 oz (175 g) linguine or other pasta	**1 oz (25 g) fresh parsley leaves**
1 tablespoon olive oil	**1 clove garlic**
1 shallot, chopped	**2 tablespoons olive oil**
1 clove garlic, chopped	**Salt and freshly milled black pepper**
6 fl oz (175 ml) dry white wine	
Salt and freshly milled black pepper	TO SERVE:
	2 tablespoons chopped fresh parsley

First prepare the pesto: select a large pan that will hold the mussels comfortably, then in it heat a tablespoon of olive oil and sauté the walnuts in the hot oil to get them nicely toasted on all sides – this will take 1–2 minutes. Place the walnuts and any oil left in the pan into a liquidizer or food processor, add the parsley and garlic, the remaining tablespoon of oil and seasoning, then blend everything to make a purée.

Next you need to deal with the mussels: heat the olive oil in the same pan that you sautéed the walnuts in, add the shallot and chopped garlic and cook these over a medium heat for about 5 minutes or until they're just soft. Now turn the heat up high, tip in the prepared mussels and add the wine and some salt and pepper. Put on a close-fitting lid, turn the heat down to medium and cook the mussels for about 5 minutes, shaking the pan once or twice or until they have all opened. Discard any that remain closed.

During those 5 minutes bring another large pan of salted water up to the boil. Then, when the mussels are cooked, remove them from the heat and transfer them to a warm bowl using a slotted spoon and shaking each one well so that no juice is left inside. Keep 8 mussels aside still in their shells, for a garnish. Then remove the rest from their shells and keep them warm, covered with foil in a low oven.

Then place a sieve lined with muslin or gauze over a bowl and strain the mussel liquor through it. This is very important as it removes any bits of sand or grit that get lodged in the shells.

Now it's time to pop the pasta into the boiling water and put a timer on for 8 minutes (some pasta might need 10 minutes so follow the instructions on the packet). Then pour the strained mussel liquor back into the original saucepan and fast-boil to reduce it by about one-third. After that turn the heat to low and stir in the pesto.

Now add the shelled mussels to the pesto sauce and remove from the heat. As soon as the pasta is cooked, quickly strain it into a colander and divide it between two hot pasta bowls. Spoon the mussels and pesto over each portion, add the mussels in their shells and scatter over the parsley. Serve absolutely immediately with some well-chilled white wine. Yummy!

CHAPTER FOUR

———————————◇———————————

POULTRY *and* THE GAME SEASON

———————◇———————

S omething that I've discovered since I last wrote about game in the *Christmas* book is the changing face of venison. Naturally lean with a low fat content, it has quite rightly come to be regarded as fashionably healthy meat, and in this country it is reared in natural herds that roam free in parklands.

Thus the emotive question of inhumane animal rearing does not apply. Because the farmed herds are controlled – which means they are culled at the right season and at the right age – we no longer have to introduce to the cooking-pot some tough and veteran trophy of the hunter that needs weeks of marinating to tenderize the flesh and has an overpowering gamey flavour. Instead, and in increasing quantities, we have tender, lean meat with a very good flavour. And it is for these reasons that I've included some new venison recipes in this chapter.

The same thing more or less could be said of pheasants which in my part of Suffolk range well and truly free (often in our garden). There's nothing to beat a well-roasted pheasant, but it *does* have to be young and tender and I must admit to having had one occasionally which turned out tough and dry. That problem shouldn't occur here because the recipes in this chapter are for alternative ways of cooking them – poaching and pot roasting.

————————————

Roast Duck with Sour Cherry Sauce

SERVES 4

T*his is a very old favourite of mine, quite nostalgic really because it was one of the first things I learned to cook when I started washing up in a restaurant. Now all these years after-wards it suddenly has taken on a whole new dimension with the arrival of dried sour cherries and some very high quality Morello cherry jams that are now available.*

1 large duck, 6 lb (2.7 kg) in weight
1 x 12 oz (345 g) jar Morello cherry jam
(with a high fruit content)
1½ oz (40 g) dried sour cherries
15 fl oz (425 ml) red wine
Salt and freshly milled black pepper
Watercress to garnish

You will also need a good solid roasting tin and either a roasting rack or a large piece of crumpled roasting foil.

Pre-heat the oven to gas mark 7, 425°F (220°C).

The most important thing to remember when you're roasting a duck is that if you like the skin really crisp it must be perfectly dry before it goes in the oven. This means if you buy it with any kind of plastic wrapping on, remove it as soon as you get it home, dry the duck thoroughly with kitchen paper and leave it in the fridge without covering, preferably for a day or so before you want to cook it.

When you're ready to cook the duck place it on a rack or on some crumpled foil in a roasting tin. Prick all the fleshy parts with a skewer, as this allows some of the fat to escape, and season it well with salt and freshly milled black pepper. Now pop it onto the highest shelf of the pre-heated oven and give it 30 minutes' initial cooking time, then reduce the heat to gas mark 4, 350°F (180°C) and con-tinue to roast the duck for a further 2 hours. From time to time during the cooking remove the tin from the oven and drain off the fat into a bowl – don't be alarmed at the amount of fat, it is quite normal and if you keep it to use later it makes wonderful roast potatoes.

Fifteen minutes before the end of the cooking time measure the wine into a jug and add the cherries to pre-soak. Then take 1 tablespoon of the jam and pass it through a sieve. Remove the duck from the oven, brush it all over with the sieved jam to make a glaze then return it to the oven for another 15 minutes.

After that, remove the duck to a carving board and let it rest for 10 minutes. Meanwhile spoon off any excess fat from the roasting tin then place it over direct heat, and stir in the wine and soaked cherries, scraping all the base and sides of the tin to incorporate all the crusty bits. Turn the heat up and let it bubble and reduce to about two-thirds of its original volume, then add 4 tablespoons of Morello cherry jam. Whisk the jam in, let it bubble and reduce for a couple of minutes more. Then carve the duck simply by using a very sharp knife to cut it into 4 sections, then pull each section away from the backbone. Spoon some of the sauce over each portion, garnish with watercress and hand the rest around the table.

NOTE: This might seem a long time to cook duck, but it's essential if you like it really crispy.

Chicken Breasts with Wild Mushroom and Bacon Stuffing and Marsala Sauce

SERVES 4

This is a very simple way to deal with four boneless chicken breasts. The use of wild porcini mushrooms combined with the beautifully rich flavour of Marsala wine in the sauce turns them into something quite unusual and special.

4 boneless, skinless chicken breasts, each weighing about 5 oz (150 g)	**Salt and freshly milled black pepper**
1 x ½ oz (10 g) pack porcini mushrooms	FOR THE SAUCE:
	5 fl oz (150 ml) dry Marsala
6 oz (175 g) open cap mushrooms, finely chopped	**1 teaspoon oil**
	Reserved pancetta
1 x 70 g pack (or 3 oz) pancetta (or streaky bacon)	**1 shallot, peeled and chopped**
	3 small mushrooms, finely sliced
1 oz (25 g) butter	**1 teaspoon chopped fresh sage leaves**
1 medium onion, finely chopped	**¾ level dessertspoon plain flour**
1 fat garlic clove, crushed	**Soaking liquid from porcini**
1 heaped teaspoon chopped fresh sage leaves	**Salt and freshly milled black pepper**
A grating of nutmeg	You will also need 4 squares of foil measuring approximately 10 inches (25.5 cm).

First you need to soak the porcini mushrooms, so pop them into a jug, pour 5 fl oz (150 ml) of boiling water over them and leave them to soak for 20 minutes. After that strain them in a sieve placed over a bowl and squeeze every last bit of liquid out of them because you are going to need it for the sauce.

Now melt the butter in a good solid frying pan, finely chop the pancetta and cook half of it in the hot butter until golden and crisp, and remove it to a plate. Then add the chopped onion to the pan and fry that gently for about 5 minutes to soften.

While that is happening, chop the strained porcini finely and add these to the pan along with the garlic, sage and finely chopped open cap mushrooms, a little nutmeg and the cooked pancetta. Stir well to get everything coated with the oil, then, as soon as the juices start to run out of the mushrooms, reduce the heat to very low and let the whole lot cook gently without covering until all the juices have evaporated and all you have left is a thick mushroom paste. This will take about 30 minutes in all. After that remove it from the heat, taste and season well with salt and freshly milled black pepper, then allow it to get completely cold.

Now take each of the chicken breasts and remove the silvery sinew from the back. Fold back the fillet, making a deeper cut if necessary, so that it opens out almost like a book. Season the chicken and spread a quarter of the mushroom mixture over it, fold back the flap and then roll it up lengthways like a Swiss roll. When they are all filled, lay each chicken breast on a lightly buttered piece of foil.

Wrap each in its foil, folding over the ends to seal. At this stage the parcels should be chilled for at least an hour to firm up.

When you're ready to cook them, pre-heat the oven to gas mark 8, 450°F (230°C). Place the chicken parcels on a baking sheet and cook for 20 minutes. Then remove them from the oven and allow them to rest, still in the foil, for 10 minutes before serving.

While the chicken is cooking you can make the sauce. First add the oil to the pan in which you cooked the mushroom filling, then gently fry the remaining pancetta and shallot for about 5 minutes, then add the sliced mushrooms and chopped sage, stir and continue to cook for about 1 minute, by which time the juices of the mushrooms will begin to run. Next stir in the flour to soak up the juices, then gradually add the porcini soaking liquid, followed by the Marsala and give a good seasoning of salt and freshly milled black pepper. Keep stirring until it bubbles and thickens, then turn the heat down and add a spoonful more of Marsala if you think it's too thick. Now let the sauce cook very gently for about 20 minutes.

To serve, unwrap each parcel onto a plate and cut each one into 4 pieces – at an angle to show the stuffing. Then pour the sauce over each one and serve straight away.

————————◇————————

Moroccan Baked Chicken with Chickpeas and Rice

SERVES 4

*C*hicken pieces simmered with chickpeas, peppers and olives in a saffron-flavoured rice with coriander and lemons – hope you like it. Chicken Basque was such a huge hit in the 'Summer Collection' because, I imagine, everything needed for a meal for four people was cooked in one large cooking pot with no extra vegetables needed. This has meant I have been under a lot of pressure to produce a recipe that could match it. So to a flourish of trumpets here it is. (See photograph on pages 72–3.)

1 x 3½–4 lb (1.5–2 kg) chicken, jointed in 8 pieces (or you could use a pack of 8 drumsticks and thighs)	3 cloves garlic, chopped
4 oz (110 g) dried chickpeas	10 fl oz (275 ml) carton good chicken stock
6 oz (175 g) brown basmati rice	5 fl oz (150 ml) dry white wine
2 fresh chillies, halved, de-seeded and finely chopped	2 oz (50 g) pitted black olives
1 rounded teaspoon cumin seeds	2 oz (50 g) pitted green olives
1 level tablespoon coriander seeds	2 tablespoons olive oil
½ teaspoon saffron stamens	Salt and freshly milled black pepper
2 x 15 g packs (or 1 oz) fresh coriander	
2 small thin-skinned lemons	
2 large yellow peppers	
2 large onions	

You will also need a wide, shallow flameproof casserole with a domed lid, about 9 inches (23 cm) across the base. Failing that, use any flameproof casserole of 5-pint (3-litre) capacity.

Pre-heat the oven to gas mark 4, 350°F (180°C).

There are two ways to deal with chickpeas. The easiest is to pop them into a bowl, cover them with cold water and leave them overnight or a minimum of 8 hours. But if it slips your mind, what you can do is place them in a saucepan, cover them with cold water and bring them up to the boil for 10 minutes. Then turn off the heat and let them soak for 3 hours. Either way, when you want to start making this recipe, the chickpeas need to be simmered for 20 minutes or until tender.

While they're simmering, place a small frying pan over direct medium heat, add the cumin and coriander seeds and toss them around in a hot pan for about 2–3 minutes or until they start to dance and change colour. Then remove the seeds to a pestle and mortar, crush them coarsely and transfer them to a plate. Next crush the saffron stamens to a powder with the pestle and mortar, then squeeze out the juice of 1 of the lemons and add it to the saffron, stirring well.

Then prepare the chicken by seasoning the joints with salt and pepper, and slice the peppers in half, remove the seeds and pith and cut each half into 4 large pieces. The onions should be sliced roughly the same size as the peppers. Now heat 1

Previous page: Moroccan Baked Chicken with Chickpeas and Rice

tablespoon of the olive oil in the flameproof casserole and when it's really hot, brown the chicken pieces on all sides – don't overcrowd the pan, it's best to do it in 2 batches, 4 pieces at a time.

After that remove the chicken pieces to a plate, then add the second tablespoon of oil and turn the heat to its highest setting. When the oil is really hot add the peppers and onions and cook them in the hot oil, moving them around until their edges are slightly blackened – this should take about 5 minutes – then turn the heat down. Strip the coriander leaves from the stalks, wrap them in a piece of cling-film and keep them in the fridge. Then chop the coriander stalks finely and add these to the peppers and onions along with the garlic, chillies, crushed spices, the chickpeas and rice, giving everything a good stir to distribute all the ingredients.

Season well with salt and pepper, then combine the lemon and saffron mixture with the stock and wine, pour it all into the casserole and stir well. Cut the remaining lemon into thin slices and push these well into the liquid. Now scatter the olives in and finally place the pieces of chicken on top of everything. Cover with a tight-fitting lid and place in the pre-heated oven for 1 hour or until the rice and the chickpeas are tender. Then just before serving scatter the coriander leaves on top, and serve straight away on warmed serving plates.

—————————◇—————————

Venison Steaks with Cranberry Cumberland Sauce

SERVES 2

This is a perfect meal for two for a special occasion, and has the added bonus of being super-fast. For Cumberland sauce redcurrant jelly is traditionally used, but when it's made with cranberry jelly, as it is here, it has a new, deliciously different dimension.

FOR THE STEAKS:	FOR THE SAUCE:
2 venison steaks, each about 7–8 oz (200–225 g)	2 rounded tablespoons cranberry jelly
1 tablespoon groundnut oil	Zest and juice of ½ large orange
1 dessertspoon crushed peppercorns	Zest and juice of ½ small lemon
2 medium shallots, finely chopped	1 teaspoon freshly grated root ginger
Salt	1 slightly rounded teaspoon mustard powder
	3 tablespoons port

Make the sauce way ahead of time – preferably a couple of hours or even several days ahead – so there is time for the flavours to develop. Take off the outer zest of half the orange and the lemon using a potato peeler, then with a sharp knife shred these into really fine hairlike strips, about ½ inch (1 cm) long.

Then place the cranberry jelly, ginger and mustard in a saucepan, add the zest and the squeezed orange and lemon juice, and place it over a medium heat. Now bring it up to simmering point, whisking well to combine everything together, then as soon as it begins to simmer turn the heat off, stir in the port and pour it into a jug to keep till needed.

When you're ready to cook the steaks, heat the oil in a medium-sized, thick-based frying pan. Dry the venison thoroughly with kitchen paper, then sprinkle and press the crushed peppercorns firmly over both sides of each steak. When the oil is smoking hot, drop the steaks into the pan and let them cook for 5 minutes on each side for medium (4 minutes for rare and 6 minutes for well done).

Halfway through add the shallots and move them around the pan to cook and brown at the edges. Then 30 seconds before the end of the cooking time pour in the sauce – not over but around the steaks. Let it bubble for a minute or two, season with salt, and then serve the steaks with the sauce poured over. A garnish of watercress would be nice, and a good accompaniment would be mini jacket potatoes and a mixed-leaf salad.

◇

Poached Pheasant with Celery
(see page 78)

Pot-Roast of Pheasant with Shallots and Caramelized Apples

SERVES 4–6

This is a superb way to cook pheasants and would make an excellent alternative Christmas lunch for four people. The pheasants are first browned and flamed in calvados (apple brandy) and then are slowly braised in cider. If you don't have any calvados you could use brandy or omit altogether. When the pheasant season comes to an end in mid-February, this works just as well with guinea fowl.

2 pheasants	**Salt and freshly milled black pepper**
1 tablespoon butter	
1 tablespoon oil	FOR THE CARAMELIZED APPLES:
12 shallots, peeled	**3 medium Cox's apples, unpeeled,**
2 fresh thyme sprigs	**quartered and each quarter sliced in 2**
1 bay leaf	**1½ oz (40 g) butter, melted**
3 tablespoons calvados	**4 oz (110 g) granulated sugar**
1½ pints (850 ml) medium cider	
1 heaped teaspoon flour and 1 heaped teaspoon butter mixed to a paste	You will also need a flameproof casserole in which 2 pheasants can sit comfortably.

Start off by heating the butter and oil together in a heavy frying pan, then brown the pheasants in the hot fat until they're a good golden colour all over. Then place them, breasts uppermost, in the casserole and season them well. Then brown the shallots in the fat remaining in the frying pan and add these to the pheasants along with the thyme and bay leaf.

Next pour the calvados into a small saucepan and warm it gently, then ignite with a match. When it is alight, pour the flaming calvados all over the pheasants. The alcohol will burn off, leaving just the beautiful essence to flavour the birds. Now pour in the cider and bring everything up to a very gentle simmer, put a tight lid on and let the pheasants braise slowly on top of the stove for 1–1¼ hours or until they're tender.

Towards the end of the cooking time, pre-heat the grill to its highest setting. Line the grill pan with foil and brush it with melted butter. Then brush each piece of apple with melted butter and dip it in sugar to coat it well all over. Place these on the foil and grill them about 2 inches (5 cm) away from the element for 6 minutes or until the sugar caramelizes, then turn them over and caramelize on the other side. When they're done they will keep warm without coming to any harm.

When the pheasants are cooked, remove them and the shallots to a warmed serving plate and keep warm. Discard the herbs, then boil the liquid in the casserole briskly without a lid until it has reduced slightly. Then whisk in the flour and butter paste with a balloon whisk, which will slightly thicken it when it comes back to the boil. Carve the pheasant and serve with the shallots and sauce poured over and garnished with the caramelized apples.

Venison Sausages Braised in Red Wine (see page 87)

Italian Stuffed Aubergines

SERVES 2 AS A LIGHT SUPPER DISH OR 4 AS A STARTER

Apart from tasting superb this is particularly pretty to look at. I like to serve it as a first course, but with a salad and some good bread it would make a lovely supper dish for two people. Strict vegetarians can replace the anchovies with an extra teaspoon of capers. (See photograph on pages 96–7.)

1 medium to large aubergine, approximately 12–14 oz (350–400 g)
3 large ripe tomatoes
1 medium onion, finely chopped
1 large clove garlic, crushed
1 tablespoon torn fresh basil leaves
2 teaspoons sun-dried tomato paste
6 drained anchovy fillets, chopped
1 rounded tablespoon drained small capers
5 oz (150 g) Mozzarella, drained

1½ level tablespoons fine fresh breadcrumbs
2 level tablespoons Parmesan (Parmigiano Reggiano), freshly grated
2 tablespoons olive oil
8 basil leaves, lightly oiled
Salt and freshly milled black pepper

You will also need a large solid baking sheet 16 x 12 inches (40 x 30 cm), lightly oiled, and a baking dish 16 x 12 inches (40 x 30 cm), also oiled.

Pre-heat the oven to gas mark 4, 350°F (180°C).

First of all wipe the aubergine and trim off the stalk end, then use the very sharpest knife you have to cut it lengthways into 8 thin slices about ¼ inch (5 mm) thick. When you get to the bulbous sides these slices should be chopped into small pieces and kept aside for the filling. Now arrange the slices of aubergine in rows on the baking sheet, then brush each slice lightly with olive oil and season with salt and pepper. Pop them into the oven on a high shelf and let them pre-cook for 15 minutes, by which time they will have softened enough for you to roll them up easily.

Next pour boiling water on the tomatoes and after 1 minute drain and slip the skins off. Then cut the tomatoes in half and, holding them in the palm of your hand, gently squeeze them until the seeds come out – it's best to do this over a plate or a bowl! Next using a sharp knife, chop the tomatoes into approximately ¼-inch (5-mm) dice. Now heat 1 tablespoon of oil in a large solid frying pan and fry the onion, chopped aubergine and garlic for about 5 minutes. Then add the chopped tomatoes, torn basil leaves and sun-dried tomato paste and continue to cook for about another 5 minutes. Give everything a good seasoning and add the chopped anchovies and capers. Then remove the pan from the heat and let the mixture cool slightly.

Now chop the Mozzarella into very small dice. As soon as the aubergines are cool enough to handle, sprinkle each one with chopped Mozzarella, placing it all along the centre of each slice. On top of that put an equal amount of stuffing ingredients, leaving a border all round to allow for expansion. Roll up the slices and put them in the baking dish, making sure the overlapping ends are tucked underneath. Finally brush each one with oil, combine the fresh breadcrumbs and Parmesan, sprinkle the mixture over them, pop a basil leaf on top, then bake in the oven (same temperature) for about 20 minutes and serve immediately.

Roasted and Sun-Dried Tomato Risotto

SERVES 2 AS A SUPPER DISH OR 3–4 AS A LIGHT LUNCH

*O*ven-roasted tomatoes, which have been slightly blackened and become really concentrated in flavour, are the mainstay of this superb dish. Add to them some sun-dried tomatoes, Parmesan, a hint of saffron and some creamy, nutty rice and you have one of the nicest risottos imaginable.

FOR THE ROASTED TOMATOES:

1½ lb (700 g) tomatoes

1 dessertspoon extra virgin olive oil

1 fat clove garlic, chopped

1 x 15 g pack (or ½ oz) basil leaves

Salt and freshly milled black pepper

FOR THE RISOTTO:

1 red onion, finely chopped

1 oz (25 g) butter

**8 oz (225 g) Italian carnaroli rice
(risotto rice)**

10 fl oz (275 ml) dry white wine

12 fl oz (330 ml) boiling water

2 teaspoons sun-dried tomato paste

**4 oz (110 g) sun-dried tomatoes,
roughly chopped**

**2 oz (50 g) Parmesan (Parmigiano Reggiano),
freshly grated, plus 1 oz (25 g) extra shaved
into flakes with a potato peeler**

¼ teaspoon saffron stamens

1 tablespoon double cream

Salt and freshly milled black pepper

You will also need a solid roasting tray 14 x 10 inches (35 x 25.5 cm), and a 9-inch (23-cm) shallow ovenproof dish of about 3-pint (1.75-litre) capacity.

Pre-heat the oven to gas mark 6, 400°F (200°C).

First of all skin the tomatoes by pouring boiling water over them, then leave them for 1 minute exactly before draining them and slipping the skins off (if they're too hot protect your hands with a cloth). Now slice each tomato in half and arrange the halves on the roasting tray, cut side uppermost, then season with salt and pepper, sprinkle a few droplets of olive oil on each one, followed by the chopped garlic, then finally top each one with half a basil leaf dipped in oil first to get a good coating.

Now pop the whole lot into the oven and roast the tomatoes for 50–60 minutes or until the edges of the tomatoes are slightly blackened. After that, remove them from the oven and then put the dish in the oven to pre-heat it, reducing the temperature to gas mark 4, 350°F (180°C) first. Now put the tomatoes and all their juices into a processor and blend. Next melt the butter in a large heavy saucepan and fry the onion for about 7 minutes until it is just tinged brown at the edges. After that add the rice and stir to coat all the grains with the buttery juices. Now crush the saffron stamens to a powder with a pestle and mortar, then add this to the rice, together with the wine. Bring it up to boiling point, let it bubble for a minute then add the tomato paste and boiling water. Give it all a good stir, season with salt and pepper and then add all the processed tomato mixture plus the dried tomatoes. Stir again and bring it just up to simmering point, then transfer the whole lot to the warm dish, return the dish to the oven and, using a timer, give it 35 minutes.

After that stir in the grated Parmesan and give it another 5–10 minutes – what you'll have to do here is to bite a grain of rice to check when it's ready. It should be tender but still retain some bite. Just before serving stir in the cream and top each portion with shavings of Parmesan and any leftover basil leaves.

Oven-Baked Wild Mushroom Risotto

SERVES 6 AS A STARTER

I've always loved real Italian risotto, a creamy mass with the rice grains 'al dente' – but oh, the bother of all that stirring to make it. Then one day I was making a good old-fashioned rice pudding and I thought, why not try a risotto in the oven?

Why not indeed – it works like a dream and leaves you in peace to enjoy the company of your friends while it's cooking. I have since discovered, in fact, that in Liguria they do make a special kind of baked risotto called 'arrosto', so my version turns out to be quite authentic after all.

½ oz (10 g) dried porcini mushrooms (see page 233)
8 oz (225 g) fresh dark-gilled mushrooms
2½ oz (60 g) butter
1 medium onion, finely chopped
6 oz (175 g) Italian carnaroli rice (risotto rice)
5 fl oz (150 ml) dry Madeira

2 tablespoons freshly grated Parmesan (Parmigiano Reggiano), plus 2 oz (50 g) extra, shaved into flakes with a potato peeler
Salt and freshly milled black pepper

You will also need a 9-inch (23-cm) shallow ovenproof dish of 2½-pint (1.5-litre) capacity, approximately 2 inches (5 cm) deep.
Pre-heat the oven to gas mark 2, 300°F (150°C).

First of all you need to soak the dried mushrooms, and to do this you place them in a bowl and pour 1 pint (570 ml) of boiling water over them. Then just leave them to soak and soften for half an hour. Meanwhile chop the fresh mushrooms into about ½-inch (1-cm) chunks – not too small, as they shrink down quite a bit in the cooking.

Now melt the butter in a medium saucepan, add the onion and let it cook over a gentle heat for about 5 minutes, then add the fresh mushrooms, stir well and leave on one side while you deal with the porcini.

When they have had their half-hour soak, place a sieve over a bowl, line the sieve with a double sheet of absorbent kitchen paper and strain the mushrooms, reserving the liquid. Squeeze any excess liquid out of them, then chop them finely and transfer to the pan to join the other mushrooms and the onion. Keep the heat low and let the onions and mushrooms sweat gently and release their juices – which will take about 20 minutes. Meanwhile put the dish in the oven to warm.

Now add the rice and stir it around to get a good coating of butter, then add the Madeira, followed by the strained mushroom-soaking liquid. Add a level tea-spoon of salt and some freshly milled black pepper, bring it up to simmering point, then transfer the whole lot from the pan to the warmed dish. Stir once then place it on the centre shelf of the oven without covering. Set a timer and give it 20 minutes exactly.

After that, gently stir in the grated Parmesan, turning the rice grains over. Now put the timer on again, and give it a further 15 minutes, then remove from the oven and put a clean tea-cloth over it while you invite everyone to be seated. Like soufflés, risottos won't wait, so serve *presto pronto* on warmed plates and sprinkle with shavings of Parmesan.

Oven-Baked Wild Mushroom Risotto

Vegetarian Moussaka with Ricotta Topping

SERVES 4–6

Yes, it is possible to make an extremely good Greek-style moussaka without meat, and even non-vegetarians will admit it tastes every bit as good. Serve it with a large bowl of crunchy salad along with some warm pitta bread.

2 aubergines, 8 oz (225 g) each	FOR THE TOPPING:
10 fl oz (275 ml) vegetable stock	**10 fl oz (275 ml) whole milk**
2 oz (50 g) Puy lentils	**1 oz (25 g) plain flour**
2 oz (50 g) green lentils	**1 oz (25 g) butter**
4 tablespoons olive oil	**¼ whole nutmeg, grated**
2 medium onions, finely chopped	**9 oz or 1 x 250 g tub Ricotta cheese**
1 large red pepper, de-seeded and chopped into ¼-inch (5-mm) dice	**1 x size 1 egg**
2 cloves garlic, peeled and crushed	**1 oz (25 g) Parmesan (Parmigiano Reggiano), freshly grated**
1 x 14 oz (400 g) tin chopped tomatoes	**Salt and freshly milled black pepper**
7 fl oz (200 ml) red wine	
2 tablespoons tomato purée or sun-dried tomato paste	
1 level teaspoon ground cinnamon	You will also need a shallow dish approximately 9 x 9 x 2½ inches (23 x 23 x 6 cm) deep.
2 tablespoons chopped fresh parsley	
Salt and freshly milled black pepper	Pre-heat the oven to gas mark 4, 350°F (180°C).

Begin by preparing the aubergines: to do this cut them into ½-inch (1-cm) dice leaving the skins on. Place them in a colander, sprinkling with a little salt between each layer, then put a small plate with a heavy weight on top – this will draw out any excess juices.

Meanwhile pour the stock into a saucepan together with the Puy lentils (but no salt), cover and simmer for 15 minutes before adding the green lentils. Cover again and cook for a further 15 minutes, by which time most of the liquid will have been absorbed and the lentils will be soft. While they're cooking heat 2 tablespoons of oil in a large solid frying pan and fry the onions until they're soft and tinged brown at the edges (about 5 minutes), then add the chopped pepper and soften and brown that too for about another 4 minutes. Next add the garlic, cook for 1 minute more, then transfer the whole lot to a plate.

Now transfer the aubergines to a clean tea-cloth to squeeze them dry, then add a further 2 tablespoons of oil to the frying pan, turn the heat up to high and toss the aubergines in it so they get evenly cooked. When they're starting to brown a little, add the drained tomatoes and the onion and pepper mixture to the pan. In a bowl mix the wine, tomato purée and cinnamon together, then pour it over the vegetables. Add the lentils and the chopped parsley, season well and let everything simmer gently while you make the topping.

All you do is place the milk, flour, butter and nutmeg in a saucepan and, using a balloon whisk, whisk until it comes to simmering point and becomes a smooth glossy sauce. Season with salt and pepper, remove it from the heat and let it cool a little before whisking in the Ricotta cheese followed by the beaten egg.

Finally transfer the vegetable and lentil mixture to the dish and spoon the cheese sauce over the top, using the back of a spoon to take it right up to the edges. Sprinkle with the Parmesan and transfer the dish to the pre-heated oven and bake on the middle shelf for 1 hour. Then allow the moussaka to rest for 15 minutes before serving.

———————◇——————

Mashed Black-Eyed Beancakes with Ginger Onion Marmalade

SERVES 4

B*lack-eyed beans are the lovely nutty beans that are popular in recipes from the deep south of America, and with the addition of other vegetables they make very good beancakes. Fried crisp and crunchy on the outside and served with this delectable Ginger Onion Marmalade, this makes a splendid vegetarian main course.*

4 oz (110 g) black-eyed beans	**1 clove garlic, chopped**
4 oz (110 g) green lentils	**¼ teaspoon ground mace**
1 pint (570 ml) water	**1 teaspoon chopped fresh thyme**
1 bay leaf	**1 tablespoon sun-dried tomato paste**
2 fresh thyme sprigs	**2 tablespoons wholewheat flour**
1 tablespoon olive oil	**4-5 tablespoons olive oil for frying**
1 red onion, finely chopped	**Salt and freshly milled black pepper**
1 medium carrot, finely chopped	
1 small red pepper, de-seeded and finely chopped	TO GARNISH:
1 green chilli, de-seeded and finely chopped	**Watercress sprigs**

First of all the black-eyed beans need soaking, this can be done by covering them with twice their volume of cold water and leaving them overnight or alternatively bringing them up to the boil, boiling for 10 minutes and then leaving to soak for 2 hours. The green lentils won't need soaking.

Once this is done, take a medium-sized saucepan, add the drained beans and the lentils, then pour in the pint of water, add the bay leaf and sprigs of thyme, then bring everything up to a gentle simmer and let them cook for about 40–45 minutes, by which time all the water should have been absorbed and the beans and lentils will be completely soft. If there's any liquid still left, drain them in a colander. Remove the bay leaf and thyme sprigs. Now you need to mash them to a pulp and you can do this using either a fork, potato masher or an electric hand whisk. After that give them a really good seasoning with salt and freshly milled black pepper and put a clean tea-cloth over them to stop them becoming dry.

Now take a really large frying pan, add the olive oil, then heat it over a medium heat and add the onion, carrot, pepper, chilli and garlic. Sauté them all together for about 6 minutes, moving them around the pan to soften and turn golden brown at the edges.

After that mix all the vegetables into the mashed bean and lentil mixture, add the mace, chopped thyme and tomato paste, then dampen your hands and form the mixture into 12 round cakes measuring approximately 2½–3 inches (6–7.5 cm) in diameter. Then place them on a plate or a lightly oiled tray, cover with cling-film and keep them in the refrigerator until needed, but for 1 hour minimum.

When you're ready to serve the beancakes, coat them lightly with wholewheat flour seasoned with salt and freshly milled black pepper, then heat 2 tablespoons of olive oil. When it is really hot reduce the heat to medium and fry the beancakes in two batches for 3 minutes on each side until they're crisp and golden, adding more oil if needed.

Drain them on kitchen paper and serve garnished with sprigs of watercress and the Ginger Onion Marmalade.

─────────── ◇ ───────────

Ginger Onion Marmalade

This is not only a wonderful accompaniment to the beancakes but is great as a relish for all kinds of other dishes — meat, fish or vegetarian.

12 oz (350 g) onions	**2 tablespoons soft dark brown sugar**
2 tablespoons olive oil	
3 rosemary sprigs	**1 rounded dessertspoon freshly grated ginger**
8 fl oz (225 ml) dry white wine	
3 tablespoons white wine vinegar	**Salt and freshly milled black pepper**

First of all, peel and slice the onions into ¼-inch (5-mm) rings (slice any really large outside rings in half). Then take a solid medium-sized saucepan and heat 2 tablespoons of olive oil. When the oil is hot, add the onions and the rosemary, stir well, and toss the onions around till they're golden and tinged brown at the edges (about 10 minutes).

After that pour in the white wine and white wine vinegar, followed by the brown sugar and the ginger, stir and bring everything up to simmering point. Add salt and pepper, then turn the heat down to low again and let everything simmer very gently for 1¼ hours or until all the liquid has almost disappeared. Then remove the rosemary, pour everything into a serving bowl and you can serve it warm — or I think it's quite nice cold with the hot beancakes.

─────────── ◇ ───────────

Gorgonzola Cheese and Apple Strudel with Spiced Pickled Pears

SERVES 6

Here is a recipe that provides something really stylish for vegetarian entertaining. Serve the strudel with the pickled pears. It's a brilliant combination of crisp pastry, melting cheese and the sharpness of the pears.

12 oz (350 g) young leeks weighed after trimming (this will be about 1½ lb/ 700 g bought weight)	**3 tablespoons chopped parsley, flat-leaf or curly**
8 oz (225 g) prepared weight of celery (reserve the leaves)	**1 oz (25 g) white bread, crust removed**
1 small Bramley apple	**2 medium cloves garlic, peeled**
1 small Cox's apple	**10 sheets of frozen filo pastry, 18 x 10 inches (45 x 25.5 cm), thawed**
8 oz (225 g) Mozzarella, cut in ½-inch (1-cm) cubes	**6 oz (175 g) Gorgonzola piccante, cut in ½-inch (1-cm) cubes**
12 spring onions, white parts only, chopped	**4 oz (110 g) butter**
1 x 3½ oz (100 g) pack ready-chopped walnuts	**Salt and freshly milled black pepper**

You will also need a large flat baking sheet approximately 16 x 12 inches (40 x 30 cm). Pre-heat oven to gas mark 5, 375°F (190°C).

First of all prepare the leeks by trimming and discarding the outer layers, then slice each one vertically almost in half and wash them under a cold running tap, fanning them out to get rid of any grit and dust. Then dry them in a cloth and cut them into ½-inch (1-cm) pieces. Now wash and chop the celery into slightly smaller pieces.

Then melt 1½ oz (40 g) of the butter in a frying pan 9 inches (23 cm) in diameter. Keeping the heat at medium, sauté the leeks and celery for about 7–8 minutes until just tinged brown, stir them and keep them on the move to stop them catching at the edges. Then tip them into a large bowl and while they are cooling you can deal with the other ingredients.

The apples need to be cored and chopped into ½-inch (1-cm) pieces, leaving the skins on, then as soon as the leeks and celery have cooled, add the apples, diced Mozzarella, spring onions, walnuts and 1 tablespoon of chopped parsley. Season everything well and stir to mix it all together.

Now you need to make a breadcrumb mixture and to do this, place the bread, garlic, the rest of the parsley and reserved celery leaves in a food processor. Switch it on and blend until everything is smooth. If you don't have a food processor, grate the bread, and chop everything else finely and mix together.

Next take a large clean tea-cloth and dampen it under cold water, lay it out on a work surface, then carefully unwrap the filo pastry sheets and lay them on the damp cloth, folding it over. It is important to keep the pastry sheets in the cloth to prevent them drying out.

It is quite complicated to explain how to assemble a strudel, but to actually *do* it is very easy and only takes a few minutes.

Place a buttered baking sheet on a work surface. Because the filo sheets are too small to make a strudel for 6 people, we're going to have to 'weld' them together. To do this, first of all melt the remaining butter in a small saucepan, then take 1 sheet of filo pastry (remembering to keep the rest covered), lay it on one end of the baking sheet and brush it with melted butter. Then place another sheet beside it overlapping it by about 2 inches (5 cm), then brush that with melted butter. Place a third sheet next to the second overlapping it again by 2 inches (5 cm).

Now sprinkle a quarter of the breadcrumb mixture all over the sheets and then place 2 more sheets of filo, this time in the opposite direction, buttering the first one with melted butter and welding the other one with a 2-inch (5-cm) join. Brush that layer as before with melted butter and repeat the sprinkling of breadcrumbs. Then place the next 3 sheets as you did the first 3, again brushing with butter and sprinkling with crumbs. Then place the final 2 sheets as the second ones and brush with butter.

After that place half the cheese and vegetable mixture all the way along the filo, sprinkle the cubes of Gorgonzola on top of that, then finish off with the rest of the mixture on top. Now just pat it together firmly with your hands. Take the edge of the pastry that is nearest to you, bring it up over the filling, then flip the whole lot over as if you were making a giant sausage roll. Neatly push in the vegetables, before tucking the pastry ends underneath. Now brush the entire surface with the remaining butter, scatter the rest of the crumb mixture over the top and bake in the oven for 25–30 minutes or until it has turned a nice golden brown colour.

To serve the strudel, cut off the ends (they are great for the bird table but not for your guests) and cut the strudel into slices, giving each person one pickled pear.

Spiced Pickled Pears

6 hard pears	**4 whole cloves**
(Conference or similar variety)	**6 juniper berries, crushed**
4 oz (110 g) soft brown sugar	You will also need a flameproof casserole
12 fl oz (330 ml) cider vinegar	approximately 10 inches (25.5 cm) in diameter,
1 tablespoon balsamic vinegar	large enough to hold the pears.
1 tablespoon whole mixed peppercorns	Pre-heat the oven to gas mark 5, 375°F (190°C).

To pickle the pears, first peel the pears using a potato peeler, but be very careful to leave the stalks intact as they look much prettier. Place all the rest of the ingredients in a flameproof casserole, bring everything up to simmering point, stirring all the time to dissolve all the sugar. Now carefully lower the pears into the hot liquid, laying them on their sides, then cover with a lid and transfer the pears to the oven for 30 minutes.

After that, remove the lid and carefully turn the pears over. Test with a skewer to see how they are cooking – they'll probably need about another 30 minutes altogether, so cover with the lid and leave them in the oven till they feel tender when pierced with a skewer. Then remove them and allow them to cool in their liquid until needed. When serving, there's no need to re-heat the pears as they taste much better cold.

THE TOP TEN CASSEROLES *and* BRAISED DISHES

◇

I remember going to a very smart, intensely stylish restaurant in the eighties and the chef telling me, rather dismissively, that if he'd known I was coming he'd have made me a casserole. Oh, if only he had! Yet such are the swings of fashion that now my old seventies favourites are back in favour with young chefs. So let us not lament the lean years of nouvelle cuisine, but rather rejoice in this decade of diversity. Back in the charts are oxtails, Irish stews, mashed potatoes, beef, lamb and pork slowly braised in lashings of sauce, real comfort foods for cold days, evoking an aura of homeliness and contentment in the kitchen to dispel the trials of the day.

If casseroles are going to make a comeback in your life, you need to convince yourself that they're really *not* a lot of work. The preparation time is never that long, and while the meal is in the oven you are left completely free – a great deal easier than standing by a grill or frying pan. The other positive side is that all casseroles improve if they're made a day ahead, cooled, refrigerated and gently re-heated when you need them. Just pre-heat the oven to gas mark 4, 350°F (180°C) and place the casserole covered in the oven for 40 minutes. So they're absolutely ideal for serving to friends: you can entertain in a much more relaxed way with no last-minute hurdles to overcome.

Still more good news is that they freeze well. If a casserole has been frozen, defrost it thoroughly then remove the cardboard lid from the foil container and replace it with double foil, and re-heat as above. In all cases make sure it has come to a gentle simmer before serving.

Pork Braised in Cider Vinegar Sauce

SERVES 4

This recipe has an autumnal ring to it and is for me the first casserole of the winter months. Pork shoulder is an excellent cut for braising and this recipe is superb for serving to friends and family, because it just cooks away all by itself until you're ready to serve it. I also think it tastes even better the next day, so if you make it that far ahead, don't add the crème fraîche until it's re-heated. The re-heating will take about 25 minutes in a casserole over gentle direct heat. Note here, though, that it's important to use a good quality cider vinegar.

2 lb (900 g) pork shoulder, trimmed and cut into 1-inch (2.5-cm) cubes	**2 bay leaves**
12 shallots, peeled	**1½ tablespoons crème fraîche**
2 tablespoons groundnut oil	**Salt and freshly milled black pepper**
½ oz (10 g) butter	
1 pint (570 ml) medium sweet cider	You will also need a wide, shallow flameproof casserole, 4-pint (2.25-litre) capacity.
5 fl oz (150 ml) cider vinegar	
4 fresh thyme sprigs	Pre-heat the oven to gas mark 3, 325°F (170°C).

First place the casserole over a fairly high heat and add half the butter and 1 tablespoon of oil. Meanwhile, dry the pieces of meat with kitchen paper then brown them a few at a time in the hot fat, transferring them to a plate as they brown.

After that add the rest of the butter and oil and when that's very hot add the shallots to the pan and carefully brown these on all sides, to a nice glossy caramel colour. Now pour the cider and cider vinegar into the pan, stir well, scraping the base and sides of the pan then return the meat, add the thyme and the bay leaves and season well.

As soon as it's all come to simmering point, transfer the casserole without a lid to the oven for approximately 1 hour and 15 minutes or until all the liquid is reduced and the meat is tender. Now remove the meat and shallots to a warm serving dish, discarding the herbs, then place the casserole back over direct heat. Bring it up to the boil and reduce the liquid to about half of its original volume. Finally whisk in the crème fraîche, taste to check the seasoning, then pour the sauce over the meat and serve. This is great served with Potato and Apple Rösti (page 154) and Spiced Sautéed Red Cabbage with Cranberries (page 155).

NOTE: If you don't have a wide *shallow* casserole, use an ovenproof dish (same size) but pre-heat it first in the oven. Make sure everything reaches simmering point in the frying pan before you pour it into the dish, then finish the sauce in a saucepan.

Braised Lamb with Flageolet Beans

SERVES 4

Though neck fillet of lamb is quite an economical cut, it provides very sweet meat that responds perfectly to long slow cooking and if you add pre-soaked dried green flageolets to cook alongside it, these too absorb all the sweet flavours of the lamb, garlic and herbs, making this an extremely flavoursome and comforting winter warmer.

2 lb (900 g) lamb neck fillets	**3 small bay leaves**
8 oz (225 g) flageolet beans	**8 oz (225 g) cherry tomatoes**
2 large onions, peeled, halved and cut into ½-inch (1-cm) rounds	**4 small fresh thyme sprigs**
2 cloves garlic, finely chopped	**2 tablespoons oil**
1 oz (25g) plain flour	**Salt and freshly milled black pepper**
1 dessertspoon chopped fresh thyme leaves	
1 pint (570 ml) supermarket lamb stock or water	

You will also need a flameproof casserole dish of approximately 4-pint (2.25-litre) capacity.

Pre-heat the oven to gas mark 1, 275°F (140°C).

You need to start this recipe off by soaking the beans. You can do this by covering the beans with twice their volume of cold water, then soaking them overnight. Alternatively, on the same day, boil them for 10 minutes then leave them to soak for a minimum of 2 hours.

When you're ready to cook the lamb, pre-heat the oven, trim off any really excess fat and then cut it into rounds about ¾ inch (2 cm) thick. Now place the casserole over direct heat, add 1 tablespoon of oil then as soon as it's smoking hot, brown the pieces of meat, a few at a time, wiping them first with kitchen paper so that they're absolutely dry when they hit the fat (don't add more than 6 pieces at a time). Then as soon as each piece is nicely browned on both sides, remove the fillets to a plate and carry on until all the meat is browned. Next add the other tablespoon of oil and, keeping the heat high, brown the onions round the edges, moving them around until they take on a nice dark caramel colour – this will take about 5 minutes – then add the garlic, stir that into the onions and let it cook for another minute or so. Now sprinkle in the flour and give it all a good stir, allowing the flour to soak into the juices. Add thyme leaves, then gradually add the stock, stirring all the while as you pour it in. Next return the meat to the casserole and season it well with freshly milled black pepper, but no salt at this stage. After that drain the beans, discarding their soaking water, and add them to the casserole as well. Finally add the thyme sprigs and bay leaves, and as soon as everything has come up to simmering point, place a tight-fitting lid on and transfer the casserole to the centre shelf of the oven. Give it 1½ hours and towards the end of that time pour boiling water over the tomatoes and then after 30 seconds drain off the water and slip the skins off. Add these to the casserole along with a good seasoning of salt, then replace the lid and carry on cooking for a further hour.

Before serving remove the bay leaves and sprigs of thyme and taste to check the seasoning.

THE TOP TEN CASSEROLES *AND* BRAISED DISHES

A Bit of the Irish Stew
with Crusted Dumplings

SERVES 4–6

This is an updated version of my 'Cookery Course' recipe, included here simply because Irish Stew is one of the best casserole dishes in the entire world. If you top it with dumplings then bake it in the oven so that they turn crusty and crunchy, you will have a heavenly banquet on your plate. Serve it as the Irish do, with simple boiled cabbage. (See photograph on pages 112–13.)

3 lb (1.35 kg) neck fillets of lamb and best end of neck cutlets mixed
2 tablespoons seasoned plain flour
12 oz (350 g) onions, thickly sliced
8 oz (225 g) carrots, cut in chunks
2 medium leeks, washed and sliced
1 large potato (about 10 oz/275 g), peeled and cut in chunks
1 rounded tablespoon pearl barley
Salt and freshly milled black pepper

FOR THE DUMPLINGS:

6 oz (175 g) self-raising flour
3 tablespoons chopped fresh parsley
3 oz (75 g) shredded suet
Salt and freshly milled black pepper

TO GARNISH:

1 tablespoon chopped fresh parsley

You will also need a 6-pint (3.5-litre) flameproof casserole.

Start off by drying the pieces of meat on kitchen paper, trim away any excess fat, cut the fillets into 1½-inch (4 cm) rounds, then dip them along with the cutlets into the seasoned flour. Now arrange a layer of meat in the base of the casserole, followed by a layer of onion, carrot, leek and potato and a good seasoning of salt and pepper. Then add some more meat and continue layering the ingredients until everything is in.

Next sprinkle in the pearl barley and pour in approximately 2 pints (1.2 litres) of hot water and bring it all up to simmering point. Spoon off any scum that comes to the surface, cover with a well-fitting lid and leave it to simmer over the lowest possible heat for 2 hours.

About 15 minutes before the end of the cooking time pre-heat the oven to gas mark 6, 400°F (200°C), then make up the dumplings. Mix the flour and parsley with a seasoning of salt and pepper in a bowl, then mix in – but do not rub in – the suet. Now add just sufficient cold water to make a fairly stiff but elastic dough that leaves the bowl cleanly. Knead it lightly then shape it into 12 dumplings.

When the stew is ready, remove the lid, place the dumplings all over the surface, then transfer the casserole to the highest shelf of the oven (without a lid) and leave it there for 30 minutes or until the dumplings are golden brown and crusty. Serve the meat surrounding the vegetables and dumplings, with some of the liquid poured over and some in a gravy boat, and sprinkle with chopped fresh parsley.

Next page: A Bit of the Irish Stew with Crusted Dumplings

CHAPTER SEVEN

A SUNDAY LUNCH REVIVAL *and* OTHER MEAT DISHES

———————◇———————

"They live well, eat and drink well, clothe warm and lodge soft...in a word the people of England eat the fat, drink the sweet, live better and fare better than the working people of any other nation in Europe. They spend more on back and belly than any other country."

So wrote Daniel Defoe in 1726. Even at the end of the century cartoonists were depicting the gulf between Europeans on a meagre diet and fat, jolly Englishmen consuming huge roast joints and vast puddings. The truth is that two centuries later we may not be seen to be eating better than other European countries but one thing that hasn't changed that much is that in Britain we are geologically geared up to rearing very good meat – the hill country of Wales and Scotland, the Lake District in the Peak District and the pastures of the West Country, where cereals won't grow.

What all this is leading up to is that because we have this special gift and because only 4.3 per cent of the population are vegetarians (from which it follows that 95.7 per cent still enjoy meat), we should celebrate it by keeping up the great British tradition of Sunday lunches. They may not be as vast as they were in the 18th century, thank goodness, but they remain an opportunity to enjoy a large joint, which can feed quite a number of people and still leave some for the next day. Cooked skilfully and lovingly, a roast is something that is unmatched anywhere in the world. I hope in the following pages you will join me in the great revival.

Roast Gammon with Blackened Crackling with
Citrus, Rum and Raisin Sauce (see page 130)

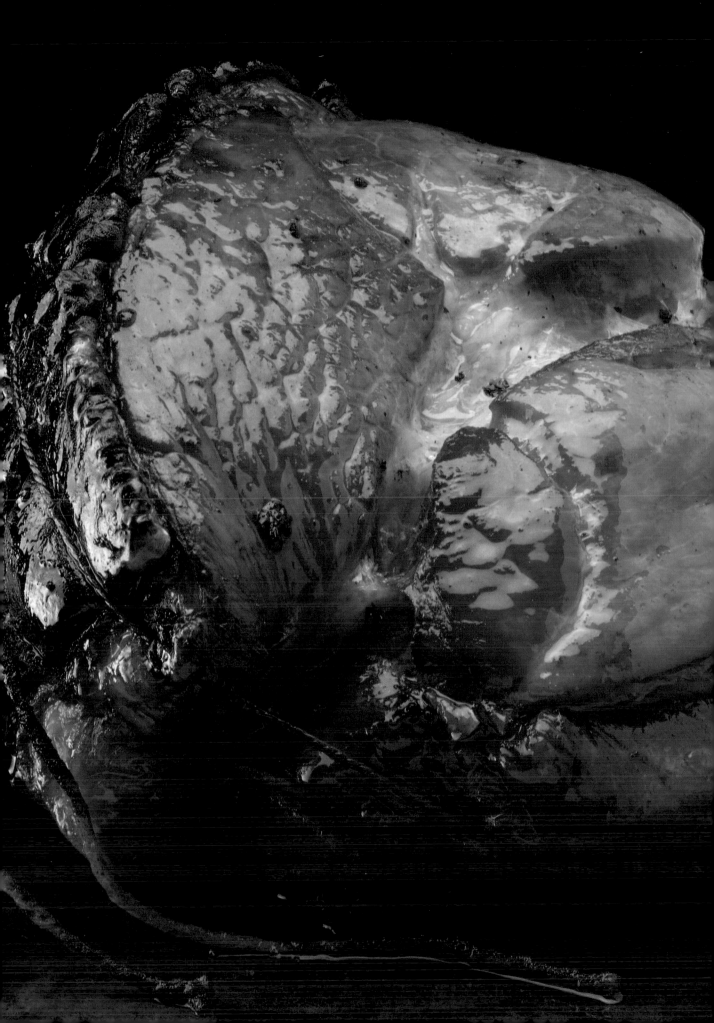

Roast Gammon with Blackened Crackling with Citrus, Rum and Raisin Sauce

SERVES 6

G*ammon is now much easier to cook than it used to be. Modern curing methods have elim-inated the need for pre-soaking, which makes it a perfect joint for roasting. If you leave the skin on, score it and paint it with black treacle, it turns into superb crackling during the cooking. It's then a very easy joint to carve, and serving it with Citrus, Rum and Raisin Sauce is a heavenly combination. If possible, always make this sweet-sharp sauce the day before you need it, so the raisins have plenty of time to absorb all the flavours and become nice and plump. (See photograph on page 129.)*

5 lb (2.25 kg) prime gammon joint, smoked or unsmoked	**3 fl oz (75 ml) dark rum**
1 level tablespoon black treacle	**3 oz (75 g) raisins**
Sea salt crystals	**4 oz (110 g) soft dark brown sugar**
	1 slightly rounded teaspoon arrowroot
FOR THE SAUCE:	
1 large juicy orange	
Zest and juice of 1 lime	You will also need a solid shallow roasting tin.

As soon as you buy the gammon remove all the wrapping and dry the skin really well with kitchen paper. After that, using a very sharp pointed knife, score the skin in a criss-cross pattern making little ½-inch (1-cm) diamonds. This is quite easy to do if you insert the tip of the knife only, then holding the skin taut with one hand drag the tip of the knife down in long movements. When you've done this place the gammon on a plate and store uncovered on the bottom of the fridge, if possible for 2 or 3 days before you need it. This means the skin will go on drying, which makes better crackling.

You can make the sauce well in advance too. All you do is remove the outer zest from the orange using a potato peeler so that you don't get any of the pith. Then pile the little strips on top of one another, and using a very sharp knife cut them into really thin needle-sized strips. If you've got the orange peel piled up and your knife is sharp this is a lot easier than it sounds. Next remove the zest from the lime, this time using a fine grater, and squeeze the juice from the lime and orange.

Place all the sauce ingredients except the arrowroot into a saucepan. Whisk the arrowroot into the mixture and place the pan onto a gentle heat, whisking all the time until it starts to simmer. As soon as this happens the sauce will change from opaque to clear, so then remove it from the heat and as soon as it is cool enough pour it into a serving dish, cover with clingfilm and chill until needed.

To cook the gammon pre-heat the oven to gas mark 9, 475°F (240°C). If the treacle is very cold, warm it slightly, then using a pastry brush or a wodge of kitchen paper lightly coat all the little diamonds of skin. After that sprinkle the skin with salt crystals, pressing them well in. Now place the gammon in a roasting tin skin-side upright (if it won't stand up straight use a couple of wedges of foil to keep it in position). Now place the roasting tin in the oven and after 25 minutes turn the heat down to gas mark 4, 350°F (180°C). Then continue to let the gammon cook for 1¾–2 hours – it should feel tender all the way through when tested with a skewer. After it comes out of the oven give it at least 30 minutes' resting time, covered with foil, in a warm place. Remove the sauce from the fridge and serve the gammon carved in slices, giving each person some crackling, and sauce spooned over.

———————— ◇ ————————

Pork Stroganoff with Three Mustards

SERVES 2

T*his is what I'd call a five-star supper dish for two people, with the added bonus that it only takes about 20 minutes to prepare from start to finish. Serve it with plain boiled basmati rice and a salad of tossed green leaves.*

12 oz (350 g) pork tenderloin	**½ oz (10 g) butter**
4 oz (110 g) small open cap mushrooms	**1 dessertspoon groundnut oil**
1 level teaspoon mustard powder	**1 small onion, halved and thinly sliced**
1 heaped teaspoon wholegrain mustard	**3 fl oz (75 ml) dry white wine**
1 heaped teaspoon Dijon mustard	**Salt and freshly milled**
1 x 200 ml tub crème fraîche	**black pepper**

First of all prepare the pork by trimming it and cutting it into little strips 3 inches (7.5 cm) long and ¼ inch (5 mm) wide. Now prepare the mushrooms by slicing them through the stalk into thin slices. Then in a small bowl mix together the 3 mustards with the crème fraîche.

When you're ready to cook the pork, take a 9-inch (23-cm) solid frying pan then heat the butter and oil together over a medium heat, add the onion slices and fry them gently for about 2–3 minutes until they are soft. Then, using a draining spoon, remove the onion to a plate, turn the heat up to its highest setting and when it's smoking hot add the strips of pork and fry them quickly, keeping them on the move all the time so they cook evenly without burning. After that add the mushrooms and toss these around to cook very briefly until their juices start to run. Next return the onion slices to the pan and stir them in. Season well with salt and pepper then add the wine and let it bubble and reduce slightly before adding the crème fraîche. Now stir the whole lot together and let the sauce bubble and reduce to half its original volume. Then serve the stroganoff immediately spooned over plain basmati rice.

———————— ◇ ————————

Autumn Lamb Braised in Beaujolais

SERVES 6–8

This is certainly one of the best ways to cook lamb in the autumn or winter months – slowly braising it under a tent of foil keeps it beautifully moist and really seems to develop its full flavour. Adding the root vegetables to cook in the braising juices is also very convenient and makes this an easy main course for entertaining. (See photograph on pages 136–7.)

1 leg of lamb, weighing 5–5½ lb (2.25–2.5 kg)	**A few fresh thyme sprigs**
4 tablespoons olive oil	**1 rosemary sprig**
1 teaspoon each chopped fresh thyme and rosemary leaves	**1 bay leaf**
	1 heaped teaspoon redcurrant jelly
1 bottle Beaujolais	**Rock salt and freshly milled black pepper**
8 small carrots, weighing about 8 oz (225 g)	
2 turnips, weighing about 8 oz (225 g)	
8 small red-skinned potatoes, weighing about 1½ lb (700 g)	TO GARNISH:
4 small parsnips, weighing about 1 lb (450 g)	**2 tablespoons chopped fresh parsley or 1 tablespoon fresh thyme leaves**
8 shallots or small onions, weighing about 8 oz (225 g)	You will also need a roasting tin approximately 14½ x 10½ inches (36 x 26 cm) and 2 inches (5cm) deep, and a large shallow roasting tray.
3 large garlic cloves, unpeeled	Pre-heat the oven to gas mark 8, 450°F (220°C).

First pour 3 tablespoons of the olive oil into the shallow roasting tray and put it into the oven as it pre-heats. Then prepare all the vegetables as follows: scrub the carrots, turnips and potatoes; top and tail the carrots and turnips, leaving the carrots whole but chopping the turnips (with skins left on) into quarters, and cut the potatoes lengthways into 4 pieces (unpeeled). Now peel the parsnips and cut them into halves; and finally peel the shallots but leave them whole.

Now dry the vegetables thoroughly in a clean tea-cloth. When the oven is up to temperature, carefully remove the roasting tray, using an oven glove to protect your hands. Place this over a direct medium heat on the hob and spoon the prepared vegetables and the unpeeled garlic into the fat. Turn them over to make sure they are well coated and return the tray to the top shelf of the oven for 25–30 minutes, turning them over at half time so that they roast evenly.

While they are in the oven, prepare the lamb by placing it in the roasting tin and rubbing the joint all over with the remaining tablespoon of olive oil, some crushed rock salt and coarsely ground black pepper.

When the vegetables are nicely tinged brown at the edges, remove them from the oven and set aside. Place the roasting tin with the lamb in the oven, on the highest shelf that will take it, and let it start to roast for 30 minutes or until it has turned a good golden colour.

Take the lamb out of the oven, then reduce the temperature to gas mark 3, 325°F (170°C) and spoon off any fat to use later. Place the roasting tin over a medium heat on top of the stove, pour in the Beaujolais and baste the meat with it. Then sprinkle with the chopped thyme and rosemary.

As soon as the wine begins to bubble, turn off the heat and cover the whole tin with a tent of foil (without it touching the meat). Fold the foil tight under the rim of the tin and replace it in the oven – on the centre shelf this time – and let it continue cooking for 1½ hours.

When the time is up, remove the roasting tin from the oven and once again transfer it to direct heat. Carefully remove the foil and baste the meat well with the wine. Spoon the browned vegetables all around in the wine, season them with salt and freshly milled black pepper and pop in the sprigs of thyme and rosemary and the bay leaf. When it has come back to simmering point, replace the foil and cook for a further 1½ hours.

After that, remove the meat and vegetables to warmed serving dishes, discarding the sprigs of herbs, then cover to keep warm. Place the roasting tin over direct heat once more and let the sauce reduce. Squeeze the garlic pulp out of the skins into the sauce and whisk this in along with a heaped teaspoon of redcurrant jelly.

Taste and season the sauce with salt and freshly milled black pepper, then pour it into a warm serving jug. Sprinkle the lamb and vegetables with the parsley or thyme and serve.

———————◇———————

Classic Roast Pork with Crackling and Roasted Stuffed Apples with Thyme and Parsley

SERVES 8

This recipe is for loin of pork which provides maximum crackling, but the butcher must chine it for you — that is, loosen the bone yet leave it attached, so that it can eventually be cut away to make carving easier.

How to get crisp, crunchy crackling is not a problem if you follow a few simple guidelines. Buy the pork a couple of days before you need to cook it, remove any plastic wrap, put it on a plate immediately and dry it as thoroughly as possible with absorbent kitchen paper. After that, leave it uncovered in the lowest part of the refrigerator, so that the skin can become as dry as possible before you start the cooking.

5 lb (2.25 kg) loin of pork, chined
1 small onion, peeled
1 tablespoon plain flour
10 fl oz (275 ml) dry cider
10 fl oz (275 ml) vegetable stock
(or potato water)

Maldon salt and freshly milled black pepper

You will also need a solid roasting tin, approximately 12 x 10 inches (30 x 25.5 cm).

Pre-heat the oven to gas mark 9, 475°F (240°C).

While the oven is pre-heating, score the skin of the pork. It will be scored already, but it's always best to add a few more lines. To do this you can use the point of a very sharp paring knife, or Stanley knife, or you can now even buy a special scalpel from a good quality kitchen shop! What you need to do is score the skin all over into thin strips, bringing the blade of the knife about halfway through the fat beneath the skin.

Now place the pork in a tin, skin-side up, halve the onion and wedge the two pieces in slightly underneath the meat. Now take about 1 tablespoon of crushed salt crystals and sprinkle it evenly over the skin, pressing it in as much as you can. Place the pork on a high shelf in the oven and roast it for 25 minutes. Turn the heat down to gas mark 5, 375°F (190°C) and calculate the total cooking time allowing 35 minutes to the pound. In this case it would be a further $2\frac{1}{2}$ hours.

There's no need to baste pork as there is enough fat to keep the meat moist. The way to tell if the meat is cooked is to insert a skewer in the thickest part and the juices that run out should be absolutely clear without any trace of pinkness. When the pork is cooked remove it from the oven and give it at least 30 minutes' resting time before carving. While that is happening, tilt the tin and spoon all the fat off, leaving only the juices. The onion will probably be black and charred, which gives the gravy a lovely rich colour. Leave the onion in, then place the roasting tin over direct heat, turned to low, sprinkle in the flour and quickly work it into the juices with a wooden spoon.

Now turn the heat up to medium and gradually add the cider and the stock, this time using a balloon whisk until it comes up to simmering point and you have a smooth rich gravy. Taste and season with salt and pepper, then discard the onion and pour the gravy into a warmed serving jug.

Serve the pork carved in slices, giving everyone some crackling and one roasted apple.

———————— ◇ ————————

Roasted Stuffed Apples with Thyme and Parsley

1 lb (450 g) good quality pork sausage meat	**8 small Cox's apples**
1 rounded dessertspoon chopped fresh parsley	**A little melted butter**
	8 small thyme sprigs
2 teaspoons chopped fresh thyme	**Salt and freshly milled black pepper**

About half an hour before the end of the cooking time of the pork, prepare the apples. First of all in a small basin mix the sausage meat, chopped parsley and thyme and add a good seasoning of salt and pepper. Using a potato peeler or an apple corer, remove the core from the apples then cut out a little more apple with a sharp knife to make the cavity slightly larger. Now divide the sausage meat mixture into 8. Then roll each portion into a sausage shape and fit that into the cavity of each apple. There will be some at the top which won't go in. So just pat that into a round neat shape. Now make a small incision around the central circumference of the apple. Brush each one with melted butter and insert a little sprig of thyme on top. Place the apples on a baking tray. Then when the pork comes out of the oven, pop the apples in to roast for about 25 minutes.

NOTE: If you're using the oven for roast potatoes and turning the heat up when the pork is cooked, the apples will cook quite comfortably on a lower shelf at the higher temperature.

———————— ◇ ————————

Next page: Autumn Lamb Braised in Beaujolais (see page 132)

Steak and Kidney Pudding

SERVES 6

I've subtitled this recipe 'Kate and Sidney make a comeback', after the Cockney slang version of this world-famous recipe. It's certainly time for a revival because it has been shamefully neglected and because it really is the ultimate in comfort food. Home-made is a far superior thing to any factory version and, believe it or not, it's dead simple to make. Once it's on the heat you can forget all about it till suppertime – except for the amazingly appetizing wafts coming out of the kitchen.

FOR THE SUET CRUST PASTRY:
12 oz (350 g) self-raising flour
6 oz (175 g) shredded beef suet
Salt and freshly milled black pepper
Cold water to mix

FOR THE FILLING:
1¼ lb (560 g) chuck steak
8 oz (225 g) ox kidney after trimming, so buy 10 oz (275 g)

2 level tablespoons well-seasoned flour
1 medium onion, sliced
Cold water
1 teaspoon Worcestershire sauce
Salt and freshly milled black pepper

You will also need a well-buttered, 2½-pint (1.5-litre) capacity pudding basin and a steamer.

To make the pastry first sift the flour and salt into a large mixing bowl. Add some freshly milled black pepper, then add the suet and mix it into the flour using the blade of a knife. When it's evenly blended, add a few drops of cold water and start to mix with the knife, using curving movements and turning the mixture around. The aim is to bring it together as a dough, so keep adding drops of water until it begins to get really claggy and sticky. Now abandon the knife, go in with your hands and bring it all together until you have a nice smooth elastic dough which leaves the bowl clean. It's worth noting that suet pastry always needs more water than other types, so if it is still a bit dry just go on adding a few drops at a time. After that, take a quarter of the dough for the lid, then roll the rest out fairly thickly. What you need is a round approximately 13 inches (32.5 cm) in diameter. Now line the bowl with the pastry, pressing it well all around. Next chop the steak and kidney into fairly small cubes, toss them in the seasoned flour, then add them to the pastry-lined basin with the slices of onion. Add enough cold water to reach almost the top of the meat and sprinkle in a few drops of Worcestershire sauce and another seasoning of salt and pepper.

Roll out the pastry lid, dampen its edges and put it in position on the pudding. Seal well and cover with a double sheet of foil, pleated in the centre to allow room for expansion while cooking. Now secure it with string, making a little handle so that you can lift it out of the hot steamer. Then place it in a steamer over boiling water. Steam for 5 hours, topping up the boiling water halfway through. You can either serve the pudding by spooning portions straight out of the bowl, or slide a palette knife round the edge and turn the whole thing out on to a serving plate (which is more fun!).

Steak and Kidney Gravy

Although steak and kidney pudding has a lovely juicy filling, it's always nice to have a little extra gravy – and since there's always some meat trimmings over, this is a good way to use them.

Meat trimmings from the steak and kidney	**1 teaspoon beef dripping**
1 onion, halved	**1 heaped dessertspoon flour**
1 pint (570 ml) water	**A few drops Worcestershire sauce**
	Salt and freshly milled black pepper

Simply place the meat trimmings in a saucepan with half the onion, cover with 1 pint of water, add some seasoning and simmer for approximately 1 hour. Then strain the stock and in the same pan fry the remaining onion, chopped small, in the beef dripping until soft and blackened at the edges. Then stir in the flour, gradually add the stock little by little to make a smooth gravy, adding a spot of gravy browning if it's needed. Taste to check the seasoning and add a few drops of Worcestershire sauce.

———————— ◇ ————————

Next page: Sunday lunch with Roast Ribs of Traditional Beef and all the trimmings (see page 142)

An Authentic Ragù Bolognese

MAKES 8 x 8 oz (225 g) PORTIONS, EACH SERVING 2 PEOPLE

*I*n Britain it's really sad that so often stewed mince with the addition of herbs and tomato purée gets presented as bolognese sauce – even, dare I say it, in lesser Italian restaurants. Yet properly made, an authentic ragù bolognese bears absolutely no resemblance to this travesty. The real thing is a very slowly cooked, thick, concentrated, dark mahogany-coloured sauce, and because of this, very little is needed to coat pasta and give it that unmistakably authentic and evocative flavour of Italy. For me making ragù is something of a ritual; it's not at all difficult, but if you give a little of your time to make it in bulk, then freeze down for the future, you'll always have the basis of a delightful meal ready-prepared when there's no time to cook.

1 lb (450 g) lean minced beef	**2 x 7 oz (200 g) tubes double concentrate tomato purée**
1 lb (450 g) minced pork	**1 x 37.5 cl half bottle red wine or 14 fl oz (400 ml)**
6 tablespoons extra virgin olive oil	
1 x 8 oz (225 g) tub chicken livers	**2 x 15 g packs (or 1 oz) fresh basil**
2 medium onions, finely chopped	**½ whole nutmeg, grated**
4 fat cloves garlic, chopped	**Salt and freshly milled black pepper**
2 x 70 g packs (or 5 oz) pancetta or streaky bacon, finely chopped	
2 x 14 oz (400 g) tins Italian chopped tomatoes	

You will also need a large flameproof casserole of 6-pint (3.5-litre) capacity.

Pre-heat the oven to gas mark 1, 275°F (140°C).

First take a large frying pan, the largest you have, heat 3 tablespoons of the oil and gently fry the onion and garlic over a medium heat for about 10 minutes, moving it around from time to time. While the onion is softening, chop the pancetta: the best way to do this after opening the pack is to roll the contents into a sausage shape, then using a sharp knife slice it lengthways into 4, then slice the lengths across as finely as possible. After 10 minutes, add this to the pan to join the onions and garlic and continue cooking them all for another 5 minutes. Now transfer this mixture to the casserole. Add another tablespoon of oil to the pan, turn the heat up to its highest then add the minced beef and brown it, breaking it up and moving it round in the pan. When the beef is browned tip it into the casserole. Heat another tablespoon of oil and do exactly the same with the minced pork. While the pork is browning, trim the chicken livers, rinse them under cold running water, dry them thoroughly with kitchen paper and chop them minutely small. When the pork is browned, transfer that to the casserole, then heat the remaining tablespoon of oil and brown the pieces of chicken liver. Add these to the casserole.

Now you've finished with the frying pan, so get rid of that and place the casserole over the direct heat, give everything a good stir together, then add the contents of the tins of tomatoes, the tomato purée, red wine and a really good seasoning of salt, pepper and nutmeg.

Allow this to come up to simmering point. Then strip the leaves from half the basil, chop them very finely and add them to the pot. As soon as everything is simmering, place the casserole on the centre shelf of the oven and leave it to cook slowly, without a lid, for 4 hours. It's a good idea to have a look after 3 hours to make sure all is well, but what you should end up with is a thick, concentrated sauce with only a trace of liquid left in it, then remove it from the oven, taste to check the seasoning, strip the leaves off the remaining basil, chop them small and stir them in.

Then when the sauce is absolutely cold, divide it, using scales, by spooning 8 oz (225 g) into polythene freezer bags. Seal them leaving a little bit of air at the top to allow room for expansion. Each 8 oz (225 g) pack, thoroughly defrosted and re-heated, will provide enough ragù for 8 oz (225 g) of pasta, which will serve 2 people.
NOTE: If you don't have a 6-pint (3.5-litre) capacity ovenproof casserole you can use a large baking dish pre-heated in the oven, but make sure everything comes up to simmering point in a large saucepan first.

Pancake Cannelloni with Ragù

SERVES 4

*I*n Umbria in Italy they make pancakes for their cannelloni, using these instead of pasta to be stuffed with ragù bolognese then topped with béchamel and Mozzarella before baking. It's a truly inspired version.

1 quantity pancakes (see page 179).

2 x 8 oz (225 g) ragù bolognese (see opposite)

FOR THE BECHAMEL SAUCE:
3 oz (75 g) grated Mozzarella cheese
1½ oz (40 g) butter
1 oz (25 g) plain flour
15 fl oz (425 ml) cold milk
Freshly grated nutmeg
Salt and freshly milled black pepper

FOR THE TOPPING:
1½ oz (40 g) Parmesan (Parmigiano Reggiano), freshly grated
1 dessertspoon olive oil

You will also need an ovenproof baking dish 10 x 8 inches (25.5 x 20 cm), 2 inches (5 cm) deep or the equivalent, well buttered.

Pre-heat the oven to gas mark 6, 400°F (200°C).

Both the pancakes and the ragù can be made well ahead and chilled or frozen. Make the béchamel sauce by the all-in-one method, that is by adding everything (except the Mozzarella) to a saucepan and whisking over a medium heat till smooth and thickened. Then continue to cook gently for 5 minutes, whisking now and then to prevent it sticking. Now lay the pancakes out and place an equal quantity (about a heaped tablespoon) of cold ragù on each one and roll up, folding in the edges. Next lay the pancakes in the ovenproof dish side by side with the ends tucked up underneath, then sprinkle over the grated Mozzarella. Pour the sauce over the top to give an even covering. Finally sprinkle over the grated Parmesan and oil and place the dish on a high shelf in the oven for 30 minutes or until the surface is golden and the sauce bubbling.
NOTE: If you want to, you could assemble all this well in advance, but make sure everything is completely cold before you cover and chill it until needed. These can also be cooked, 3 pancakes per person, in individual ovenproof dishes – in which case cut the cooking time to 20 minutes.

Timings for One O'Clock Lunches for Eight

Sunday traditional lunches for eight guests with no last-minute panics. Impossible?
Not if you follow these straightforward timings.

ROAST RIBS OF BEEF	PERFECT ROAST POTATOES	COMPOTE OF GLAZED SHALLOTS	TRADITIONAL YORKSHIRE PUDDING
SEE PAGES 142–3	SEE PAGE 149	SEE PAGE 160	SEE PAGE 143
6 lb (2.7 kg) Rib Joint (or Sirloin) Timings below are for beef cooked to medium. 9.30 am Place the beef in the oven, lower the oven temperature after 30 minutes, baste three times during roasting. 12 noon Remove the meat from the oven, cover loosely with foil and keep warm. Increase the oven temperature for the roast potatoes. Meat cooking time: 2½ hours. Adjust cooking times Rare: 2 hours Medium rare: 2¼ hours Well done: 2¾ hours	12.10 pm Place the prepared potatoes in the oven on a high shelf for 40–50 minutes.	11.45 am Place the prepared shallots onto a gentle heat for 1 hour 15 minutes.	12.20 pm Place the Yorkshire Pudding on the middle shelf for 40 minutes. GRAVY Make the gravy at 12.45 pm.

TRADITIONAL ROAST CHICKEN	PERFECT ROAST POTATOES	SAUTEED CARAMELIZED FENNEL	GIBLET GRAVY
SEE PAGES 76–7	SEE PAGE 149	SEE PAGE 158	Make at 12.45 pm.
2 x 4lb (1.8 kg) chickens 10.45 am Place them in the oven, baste every 30 minutes. 12 noon Raise the oven temperature to gas 7, 425°F (220°C). 12.30 pm Remove the chickens from the oven. Keep them warm. Cooking time: 1¾ hours.	12.10 pm Place the prepared potatoes on shelf above the chickens for 40–50 minutes.	(1½ times recipe) 12 noon Steam the fennel. 12.10 pm Place the fennel over direct heat for 40–50 minutes. STEAMED BROCCOLI Cooking time: 8 minutes.	

ROAST GAMMON WITH BLACKENED CRACKLING SEE PAGES 130–1 5 lb (2.25 kg) Gammon Joint 9.45 am Place the gammon in the oven, reducing the oven temperature after 25 minutes. 12 noon Raise the oven to gas 7, 425°F (220°C). 12.10 pm Remove the gammon from the oven, keeping it warm and loosely covered with foil. Cooking time: 2½ hours.	**PERFECT ROAST POTATOES** SEE PAGE 149 12.10 Place the prepared potatoes in the oven on a high shelf for 40–50 minutes.	**SPICED SAUTEED RED CABBAGE** SEE PAGE 155 You will need 1½ times the recipe. Pre-cook the cabbage at a convenient time during the morning. 12.50 pm Re-heat gently for 8–10 minutes.	**CITRUS, RUM AND RAISIN SAUCE** SEE PAGE 130 Make at a convenient time in the morning. Chill until needed.
CLASSIC ROAST PORK WITH CRACKLING SEE PAGES 134–5 5 lb (2.25 kg) Loin of Pork (chined). 9.45 am Place the pork in the oven. 12 noon Raise the oven temperature to gas 7, 425°F (220°C). 12.15 pm Remove the pork from the oven and keep warm. Cooking time: 2½ hours.	**PERFECT ROAST POTATOES** SEE PAGE 149 12.10 Place the prepared potatoes in the oven on a high shelf for 40–50 minutes. 12.40 pm Place the stuffed apples on a low shelf for 20 minutes. (They will cook at this slightly higher temperature quite comfortably if you are using the oven for roasted potatoes.)	**COMPOTE OF GLAZED SHALLOTS** SEE PAGE 160 11.45 am Place the prepared shallots onto a gentle heat for 1 hour 15 minutes.	**BRUSSELS SPROUTS** Choose small, tight Brussels, trimmed. Make a cross-like incision at the stalk end. Steam or boil for 5–8 minutes, drain (reserve liquid for gravy). Toss in a little hot, melted butter. 12.50 pm Make the gravy.
AUTUMN LAMB BRAISED IN BEAUJOLAIS SEE PAGES 132–3 5–5½ lb (2.3–2.5 kg) Leg of Lamb 8.45 am Vegetables in oven to brown, 30 minutes, turn them over halfway. 9.15 am Lamb in oven, lower the temperature after 30 minutes.	11.15 am Add the browned vegetables to lamb. 12.45 pm Remove lamb and vegetables, keep warm, finish the sauce. Cooking time: 3½ hours.		

CHAPTER EIGHT

WINTER VEGETABLE SELECTION

———◇———

While I welcome the new varieties of salad ingredients from around the world that can enliven our winter salads, I have to admit I'm not such a great fan of imported vegetables. I enjoy summer vegetables in the summer and early autumn and after that I'm quite happy to forget about them and look forward to whatever winter has to offer: onions, young leeks, shallots, tiny button Brussels sprouts, crisp squeaky cabbages, fragrant celery. And I love all the roots – celeriac, carrots, swedes, turnips, Jerusalem artichokes and, best of all, parsnips.

First and foremost I think we need to enjoy all these wonderful vegetables simply as they are, especially when they are accompanying dishes with lots of strong, rich flavours. Let us not underestimate simple boiled cabbage, or leeks cooked just in their own juices with a knob of butter, or a dish of carrots steamed then chopped small with a seasoning of black pepper – one of my particular favourites. However, the winter vegetable season does seem to go on for a long time and the limited varieties may get a bit repetitive, so it's also a good time to experiment with new ideas for cooking them, and I hope that's what you'll find on the following pages.

Because of the enormous popularity of oven-roasting vegetables in the *Summer Collection* and seeing how liberating it is when you have to attend to other parts of the meal, I have included here new ideas for oven-roasting winter vegetables along the same lines. This chapter also celebrates the recent revival of mashed potato, which offers all kinds of variations and, when made carefully, is one of the real joys of winter.

———————————————

Perfect Roast Potatoes

SERVES 8

The amounts here are not vital because it depends on who's greedy and who is on a diet and so on, but I find that 8 oz (225 g) per person is enough – yielding three each and a few extras for inevitable second helpings! I like Désirée best of all, but my second choice would be Romano.

4 lb (1.8 kg) Désirée potatoes
4 oz (110 g) dripping or lard
Salt

You will also need a shallow solid roasting tray 16 x 12 inches (40 x 30cm).

Pre-heat the oven to gas mark 7, 425°F (220°C).

First place the roasting tray with the fat in it on the highest shelf of the oven while it pre-heats. Thinly peel the potatoes using a potato peeler, then cut them into fairly even-sized pieces, leaving the small ones whole. Then place them in a saucepan, pour over boiling water from a kettle, just to cover, then add salt and simmer for about 10 minutes. After that lift one out with a skewer and see if the outer edge is fluffy. You can test this by running the point of the skewer along the surface – if it stays smooth, give it a few more minutes.

Then drain off the water, reserving some for the gravy. Place the lid back on the saucepan, and, holding the lid on firmly with your hand protected by a cloth or oven-glove, shake the saucepan vigorously up and down. This shaking roughens up the cooked edges of the potato and makes them floury and fluffy – this is the secret of the crunchy edges.

Now, still using the oven-glove to protect your hands, remove the hot roasting tray containing its sizzling fat and transfer to the direct heat (medium) on the hob. Then use a long-handled spoon and quickly lower the potatoes into the hot fat. When they are all in, tilt the tray and baste each one so it's completely coated with fat. Now place them back on the highest shelf of the oven and leave them unattended for 40–50 minutes or until they are golden brown. There's no need to turn them over at half-time – they will brown evenly by themselves. Sprinkle them with a little crushed salt before serving straight away; they lose their crunch if you keep them waiting. If they're ready before you are, turn the oven off and leave them inside.

◇

Potato and Apple Rösti

SERVES 4

This is extremely good served with pork dishes and really meaty pork sausages. I think it goes particularly well with the Pork Braised in Cider Vinegar Sauce on page 109. If you're cooking it for friends, it can all be made in advance and kept in the refrigerator until needed. And the best news of all is it gets cooked in the oven so there's no last-minute fuss and bother with frying.

2 medium-sized Désirée or Romano potatoes (about 10 oz/275 g)	**1 level tablespoon flour**
2 medium Granny Smith apples	**2 oz (50 g) melted butter**
2 tablespoons fresh lemon juice	**Salt and freshly milled black pepper**
Freshly grated nutmeg	You will also need a solid ovenproof baking tray 14 x 10 inches (35 x 25.5 cm).

First of all place the scrubbed whole potatoes in a saucepan, add some salt and enough boiling water to just cover, then boil them for 8 minutes (it's important not to over-boil them). Then drain off the water and while they are cooling you can deal with the apples.

First place the lemon juice into a shallow dish, then peel, core, quarter and grate the apples using the coarse side of a grater placed directly over the bowl. When all the apple is grated, quickly toss it well in the lemon juice to prevent it turning brown.

Now peel the potatoes and grate them in the same way, but this time letting the shreds fall into a large bowl. Now transfer the apple to join the potato, squeezing it in your hand to leave any surplus juice behind. Give everything a good seasoning of salt, pepper and some nutmeg and toss the two together to combine them as evenly as possible.

Now using your hands, shape the mixture into 8 small rounds about 2½ inches (6 cm) in diameter, squeezing firmly to form little cakes that have nice raggedy edges. As you make the little rösti cakes, place them on a plate, then put the flour on another small plate. Dust each cake lightly with flour, return it to the first plate, then cover them all with clingfilm. They can now sit happily in the fridge for up to 6 hours or until needed.

When you're ready to cook the rösti, pre-heat the oven to gas mark 7, 425°F (220°C). Brush the roasting tray with the melted butter, place the little rösti cakes on the tray and brush the tops with melted butter. When the oven is up to heat, pop them on a high shelf, give them 10 minutes using a timer, then using a fish slice turn them over and give them another 10–15 minutes, by which time they will be crisp and golden on the outside, cooked through and ready to serve.

───────◇───────

Previous page: Roasted Roots with Herbs (see page 161)

Spiced Sautéed Red Cabbage with Cranberries

SERVES 4–6

I have always adored red cabbage cooked long and slow, but it's also extremely good cooked fast so that it retains some bite and crunchiness. Using cranberries rather than the usual apples gives this dish a jewel-like appearance and their sharp flavour gives an edge to the spiciness.

1 lb (450 g) red cabbage, cut into 4 sections and cored	1 heaped dessertspoon soft brown sugar
1 dessertspoon groundnut oil	1½ tablespoons red wine vinegar
1 medium onion, chopped	4 oz (110 g) cranberries
1 large garlic clove, finely chopped	Salt and freshly milled black pepper
⅓ level teaspoon powdered cloves	
⅓ rounded teaspoon powdered cinnamon	
⅓ whole nutmeg, freshly grated	

You will also need a very large frying pan or, even better, a wok.

First of all you need to shred the cabbage quite finely into ¼-inch (5-mm) shreds, discarding any tough stalky bits. Now heat the oil in the pan over a medium heat, stir in the onion, cook it for 2–3 minutes, then add the garlic and continue to cook for another 2–3 minutes. Then turn the heat up to its highest setting and add the cabbage. Using a wooden spoon, keep the cabbage constantly on the move, so it comes into contact with the hot pan on all sides.

After about 3–4 minutes of cooking, still stirring, sprinkle in the spices, a seasoning of salt and pepper followed by the cranberries. Then turn the heat down and let it go on cooking for a further 5–10 minutes, stirring it once or twice during that time. Bite a piece to see if it's tender, then when it's ready turn the heat up again, sprinkle in the sugar and vinegar, give it all a few more good stirs and then it's ready to serve.

NOTE: If you're careful not to overcook it in the beginning, you can prepare this in advance and just quickly heat it up for serving.

◇

Celery Baked in Vinaigrette with Pancetta and Shallots

SERVES 2

T*his is a great way to serve celery as a vegetable. I used greaseproof paper for this in the photo-graph opposite, as it looks very pretty if you take the whole parcel to the table – otherwise foil would do.*

1 head celery	**1 dessertspoon white wine vinegar**
6 shallots, peeled (and split if the bulbs are dividing)	**Salt and freshly milled black pepper**
1 or 2 thyme sprigs	
1 rosemary sprig	
4 sage leaves	You will also need a double thickness of greaseproof paper, 15 x 24 inches when folded (38 x 60 cm), and a large solid baking tray.
3 slices pancetta or smoked streaky bacon	
3 tablespoons light olive oil	Pre-heat the oven to gas mark 9, 475°F (240°C).

Begin by removing the tough outer layers of the celery, then pare the outside of the root off, but leave it attached. Now cut across the celery about 3½ inches (9 cm) from the base. Stand the lower half upright and cut vertically through the centre. Then cut each half into 4 to make 8 pieces, keeping them attached to the root. Save a couple of nice leaves (preferably attached to a small stem) and trim the top pieces of celery to a similar length to the base, cutting off any really tough and stringy edges. Now wash all the pieces and dry them on kitchen paper.

Next heat 1 tablespoon of the oil in a frying pan, then lightly brown the celery and shallots, keeping them on the move so they brown evenly. Now transfer them to a plate. Increase the heat under the pan, add the pancetta and fry the slices until they're really crisp – it will take 2–3 minutes and you'll need to keep turning them.

Next lay the greaseproof paper over the baking tray and lightly grease a circle of 9 inches (23 cm) on it. Arrange the celery in an attractive shape on the paper, putting the prettiest pieces on the top, add the shallots, thyme, rosemary and sage leaves in among it, and season with salt and pepper.

Now combine the remaining olive oil and wine vinegar, sprinkle that over the vegetables, followed by the pancetta crumbled into pieces with your hands. Next fold the greaseproof paper over and seal, making pleats, all round – you may find a couple of metal (not plastic) paper clips useful here, as it's essential to keep the steam trapped inside. Place the parcel in the pre-heated oven for 20–25 minutes.

After that carefully unwrap the paper – you may need scissors – and serve the vegetables with the juices spooned over.

NOTE: For 4 to 6 people, double the ingredients and make 2 parcels.

⎯⎯⎯⎯⎯ ◇ ⎯⎯⎯⎯⎯

Celery Baked in Vinaigrette with Pancetta and Shallots

Sautéed Caramelized Fennel

SERVES 4–6

4 medium-sized heads fennel

1 oz (25 g) butter

1 rounded teaspoon granulated sugar

10 fl oz (275 ml) medium cider

2 fl oz (55 ml) cider vinegar

Salt

You will need a wide saucepan with a lid, about 9–10 inches (23–25.5 cm) in diameter, into which the trimmed fennel will fit snugly.

To prepare the fennel bulbs, first cut off the leafy fronds and reserve them for a garnish. Now trim off the green shoot by cutting diagonally to make a V-shape. Then slice off the root part at the other end, keeping the bulb intact, and remove any tough or brown outer layers, then slice across each bulb to cut it in half.

Then place the fennel in a fan steamer set in the saucepan with 1 inch (2.5 cm) of boiling water under it. Cover and steam for 10 minutes then remove them from the steamer, throw out the water, wipe the inside of the pan with kitchen paper and return it to the heat.

Next melt the butter and sugar in the saucepan and when it starts to foam, stir it around the pan until the sugar dissolves, then add the fennel, cut side down. Keeping the heat fairly high, brown it for 5 minutes then turn the pieces over and brown them on the other side for another 3 minutes.

Now combine the cider, cider vinegar and a little salt and pour this into the pan, then keeping the cut side of the fennel facing upwards, cover with a lid and simmer gently for 20 minutes. After that turn the fennel over again. Then continue to cook for a further 20–25 minutes (this time uncovered). Watch carefully during the last 10 minutes and test to see if it is cooked by inserting a skewer.

When the fennel is tender enough, raise the heat so that the remaining juices reduce to a glaze. Shake the pan carefully to give an even covering of the caramel glaze. Now transfer the whole lot to a warm serving dish with the cut surfaces upwards and scatter with the chopped fennel fronds as a garnish.

◇

Oven-Roasted Cauliflower and Broccoli with Garlic and Coriander

SERVES 4

These two particular vegetables can become a bit repetitive as winter wears on, so here's a deliciously different way to cook them – no water, just in the heat of the oven, which concentrates their flavour wonderfully.

8 oz (225 g) cauliflower	**2 garlic cloves, peeled**
8 oz (225 g) broccoli	**Salt and freshly milled black pepper**
2 tablespoons olive oil	
1 heaped teaspoon whole coriander seeds, coarsely crushed	You will also need a large solid roasting tray.

Pre-heat the oven to gas mark 6, 400°F (200°C).

All you do is trim the cauliflower and broccoli into florets, 1 inch (2.5 cm) in diameter, and place them in a mixing bowl, then sprinkle in the crushed coriander seeds. Crush the cloves of garlic together with ¾ level teaspoon salt in a pestle and mortar until you have a paste. Whisk the oil into this, then pour the whole mixture over the broccoli and cauliflower. Use your hands to toss and mix everything together to get a nice coating of oil and coriander, then arrange the florets on the roasting tray and season with salt and pepper. Bake for 25–35 minutes or until tender when tested with a skewer, and serve straight away.

──────── ◇ ────────

Compote of Glazed Shallots

SERVES 8

T*his recipe is dead simple, yet it draws out all the sweet, fragrant flavour of the shallots and at the same time gives them a glazed pink, jewel-like appearance. These make an excellent partner to beef or you can add a bit of sophistication to bangers and mash. Also, cider and cider vinegar can be used instead of wine to make it more economical.*

1½ lb (700 g), approximately 24 small, even-sized shallots, peeled and left whole (ones that split into twins count as 2)	2 fl oz (55 ml) red wine vinegar
	14 fl oz (400 ml) dry red wine
	1 teaspoon sugar
	Salt

Use a wide, shallow saucepan which will take the shallots in one layer, then simply place all the above ingredients except the sugar in it and bring everything up to simmering point. Then turn the heat down to its lowest setting and let the shallots simmer (just a few bubbles breaking the surface) for 1–1¼ hours. Turn the shallots over at half-time, and 10 minutes before the end of the cooking time sprinkle in the sugar. You should end up with tender shallots glistening with a lovely glaze. If your heat source is not low enough, you may need to use a diffuser. If it's more convenient you can cook the shallots in advance, and gently re-heat them before serving.

———————— ◇ ————————

Roasted Roots with Herbs

SERVES 4

Since oven-roasted vegetables in the 'Summer Collection' were so very popular, I simply had to do a winter version. Here it is and once again it's a winner for entertaining, not least because all the vegetables get cooked together with little or no attention. (See photograph on pages 152–3.)

½ swede (about 5 oz/150 g), cut into 1-inch (2.5-cm) wedges	1 fat garlic clove, crushed
4 small whole carrots	3 tablespoons olive oil
4 small whole parsnips	1 tablespoon chopped mixed herbs (including thyme, rosemary and sage)
1 small turnip, cut in half and then into ¾-inch (2-cm) slices	Salt and freshly milled black pepper
2 medium red onions, peeled and cut through the root into quarters	
2 red potatoes, 5 oz (150 g) each, cut into 6 wedges	

You will also need a solid baking sheet 16 x 12 inches (40 x 30 cm).

Pre-heat the oven to its highest setting.

First scrub the carrots and parsnips, dry them well and place them in a large bowl with all the other prepared vegetables. Now add the crushed garlic, olive oil and mixed herbs, then using your hands, mix well to make sure they all have a good coating of the oil. You can leave them like this covered with clingfilm for up to 2 hours until you are ready to cook them – in which case the oil will have nicely absorbed the flavour of the garlic and herbs.

Then arrange them on the baking sheet, sprinkle with salt and a good grinding of black pepper and cook in the pre-heated oven on a high shelf for 35–40 minutes or until they are cooked through.

◇

Hung Shao Pork with Stir-Fry Greens

SERVES 2

I t must have been about 20 years ago that I first met Ken Lo, the famous cookery writer and restaurateur, and asked him how to make this, which is one of my favourite Chinese dishes. He didn't just give me the recipe, he came round to the flat where we were living and cooked it, giving us a lesson on the principles of Chinese cookery at the same time. The great thing about this recipe, which is still a huge favourite, is that it transforms an inexpensive piece of streaky pork roast into something exotic and unusual.

1 lb (450 g) lean belly pork, including the skin (buy it as a whole piece)
4 tablespoons dark soy sauce
1 tablespoon water
1 dessertspoon finely chopped fresh ginger
1 star anise
2-inch (5-cm) piece cinnamon stick, broken into shreds
1 teaspoon sugar
3 tablespoons dry sherry
Salt

FOR THE STIR-FRY VEGETABLES:
4 oz (110 g) broccoli
4 oz (110 g) Savoy cabbage
1 large leek
1-inch (2.5-cm) piece fresh ginger
1 large garlic clove
2 spring onions
1 tablespoon dark soy sauce
2 tablespoons dry sherry
2 tablespoons water
2 tablespoons groundnut oil

You will also need a medium-sized flameproof casserole, plus a wok or a large frying pan.

First of all prepare the pork. What you need to do is cut it into 1-inch (2.5-cm) cubes, making quite sure that each piece still has the skin attached. You don't have to eat the skin, but its gelatinous properties are very important to the flavour of the finished dish. Now arrange the pieces of pork, skin-side down, in a small flame-proof casserole and sprinkle them with a little salt and then with the soy sauce and the water. Next add the chopped ginger, sprinkling it all around, popping in the star anise and the cinnamon as well. Now cover the casserole, turn on the heat and as soon as the juices start to simmer, turn the heat down to its lowest possible setting and cook the pork for 45 minutes. After that turn the pieces of pork over on to their other side, sprinkle in the sugar and the sherry, then cover again and continue to cook very slowly for a further 45 minutes, turning the meat over once or twice more during that time.

Towards the end of the cooking time, prepare the vegetables. To do this, first cut off the flowery heads of the broccoli, separating them and slicing them into small pieces. Then cut the stalky bits diagonally into very thin slices. The cabbage needs to be de-stalked and sliced thinly and the leek cleaned, halved lengthways and cut diagonally into slices. Peel the piece of ginger and slice this into little matchstick strips, and do the same with the garlic. Then chop the white part of the spring onions into thin rounds and the tender, green part into matchstick pieces.

Now, in a little jug, mix together the soy sauce, sherry and water. Then about 3 minutes before the pork is ready, heat up a wok or a large frying pan until it is very hot. Then add the oil and, when that's hot, add the ginger and garlic, tossing it about for 30 seconds. After that add the broccoli. Then add the cabbage, leek and the green part of the spring onion.

Stir-fry this for about 1 minute, then finally add the rest of the spring onion and the soy sauce mixture. Then give it another few seconds, tossing and stirring, then serve the vegetables and the pork on a bed of plain boiled rice with any juices left in the wok poured over.

———————◇———————

Marinated Cucumber and Sesame Salad

SERVES 2

If you're serving Teriyaki Steak (see page 174), I think it's nice to have something cool and crunchy to go with it. This very simple salad makes a nice little side dish. I also like to serve it as a nibble before an oriental meal.

½ cucumber	1 teaspoon mirin
1 rounded tablespoon white sesame seeds	1 teaspoon saké
	1 teaspoon rice vinegar
1½ tablespoons soy sauce	½ teaspoon sugar

First of all begin by toasting the sesame seeds. Do this by using a small, solid frying pan, pre-heat it over a medium heat, then add the sesame seeds and toast them, moving them around in the pan to brown them evenly. As soon as they begin to splutter and pop and turn golden, they're ready. This will take about 1–2 minutes. Then remove them from the frying pan to a plate. Next cut the cucumber in half lengthways, then in quarters and then in eighths. Remove the seeds, chop into small, 1½-inch (4-cm) wedges, then place them in a bowl. After that measure the soy sauce, mirin, saké, rice vinegar and sugar into a screw-top jar, shake them together thoroughly, then pour them over the cucumber and leave to marinate for about 1 hour, giving them one good stir at half-time. Just before serving lightly crush the sesame seeds with a pestle and mortar and sprinkle them over the salad.

———————◇———————

Singapore Stir-Fried Noodles

SERVES 2

*O*nce again I have to thank Ken Lo for introducing me to this incredibly good recipe, which is a spectacular combination of flavours, textures and colours. If you can't get dried Chinese mushrooms or shrimps (see page 235) use more of the fresh ones and it will still be wonderful.

4 oz (110 g) rice noodles	**½ teaspoon salt**
6 Chinese dried mushrooms	**2 oz (50 g) cooked chicken or pork, finely shredded**
1 heaped tablespoon Chinese dried shrimps	**2 oz (50 g) peeled prawns, chopped into thirds**
2 tablespoons groundnut oil	**2 tablespoons mushroom soaking water**
1 medium onion, chopped small	**1½ tablespoons soy sauce (Japanese is best)**
2 rashers streaky bacon, chopped small	**4 spring onions, finely chopped, including green parts**
1 large garlic clove, chopped	**2 tablespoons dry sherry**
1 heaped teaspoon freshly grated ginger	
1 dessertspoon Madras curry powder	You also need a wok or very large frying pan.

First of all you need to soak the dried mushrooms and shrimps – to do this place them in a jug and pour boiling water over them and leave them aside to soak for 30 minutes. Meanwhile you can get on with all the chopping of the other ingredients.

After the mushrooms and shrimps have soaked, drain off the water, reserving it for later. Give the mushrooms a squeeze and chop them into fine shreds. Now place the noodles in a large bowl, cover them with warm water and leave them to soak for 15 minutes.

Next heat the oil in the wok and when it's very hot add the onions, mushrooms, soaked shrimps, chopped bacon, garlic and ginger. Stir them round in the hot oil, then reduce the heat and gently let all the ingredients cook together for about 15 minutes. This initial slow cooking allows all the delicious flavours and aromas to permeate the oil.

After 15 minutes add the curry powder and salt to the cooked ingredients, then drain the noodles in a colander – give them a really good shake to get rid of any excess water. Then turn the heat under the pan up to medium, add the chicken, then the fresh prawns, followed by the chopped spring onion. Next add the drained noodles to the pan, then using either a large fork or some chopsticks toss the ingredients around so that everything is incorporated amongst the noodles. Finally sprinkle in the combined soy sauce, mushroom water and sherry, give everything a good stir and serve immediately on hot plates.

––––––––––– ◇ –––––––––––

Pears Baked in Marsala Wine

SERVES 8

The rich, dark flavour of Marsala combined with fragrant pear juices is a quite stunning combination. When you shop for the pears, looks are important: a good pear shape and a long stalk intact are essential, and the fruit needs to be hard and not ripe – which is perhaps fortunate as ripe pears always seem difficult to find.

FOR THE PEARS:	TO SERVE:
8 large hard pears	**1 x 500 ml tub crème fraîche**
1 pint (570 ml) Marsala	
2 oz (50 g) caster sugar	You will also need a large flameproof casserole
2 whole cinnamon sticks	with a tight-fitting lid.
1 vanilla pod	
1 rounded dessertspoon arrowroot	Pre-heat the oven to gas mark ½, 250°F (130°C).

Using a potato peeler thinly pare off the outer skin of the pears, but leave the stalks intact. Then slice off a thin little disc from each pear base so they can sit upright. Now lay the pears on their side in the casserole. Pour in the Marsala then sprinkle over the sugar and add the cinnamon sticks and vanilla pod.

Now bring everything up to simmering point, then cover the casserole and bake the pears on a low shelf in the oven for about 1½ hours. After that remove the casserole from the oven, turn the pears over onto their other side, then replace the lid and return them to the oven for a further 1½ hours.

When the pears are cooked, transfer them to a serving bowl to cool, leaving the liquid in the casserole. Then remove the cinnamon sticks and vanilla pod. Place the casserole over direct heat and then, in a cup, mix the arrowroot with a little cold water until you have a smooth paste. Add this to the casserole, whisking with a balloon whisk as you add it. Bring the syrup just up to simmering point, by which time it will have thickened slightly. Then remove from the heat and when the syrup is cool, spoon it over the pears, basting them well.

Now cover the pears with foil or clingfilm and place them in the fridge to chill thoroughly. Serve the pears sitting upright in individual dishes with the sauce spooned over and the crème fraîche handed round separately.

NOTE: This recipe can also be made, as in the photograph opposite, with red wine or strong dry cider – each version has its own particular charm.

————————————— ◇ —————————————

Pears Baked in Marsala Wine, Red Wine and Dry Cider

Banoffee Cheesecake with Toffee Pecan Sauce

SERVES 6–8

The magic word 'banoffee' does not, as you might have thought, have exotic origins: it is simply an amalgam of banana and toffee. But it is magic nonetheless – the combination of bananas, cream and toffee is inspired. Here I have incorporated them all into a cheesecake with the addition of one extra star ingredient, toasted pecan nuts.

FOR THE BASE:

4 oz (110 g) sweet oat biscuits

1½ oz (40 g) melted butter

3 oz (75 g) pecan nuts (use half for the base and half for the sauce – see below)

FOR THE FILLING:

3 medium-size ripe bananas, 8 oz (225 g) peeled weight

1 tablespoon lemon juice

3 x size 1 eggs

12 oz (350 g) medium fat curd cheese

1 x 200 g tub fromage frais (8% fat)

6 oz (175 g) caster sugar

FOR THE SAUCE:

2 oz (50 g) butter

3 oz (75 g) soft brown sugar

2 oz (50 g) granulated sugar

5 oz (150 g) golden syrup

5 fl oz (150 ml) double cream

A few drops vanilla extract

FOR THE TOPPING:

3 medium-size ripe bananas

2 tablespoons lemon juice

You will also need a springform cake tin, 8 inches (20 cm) in diameter, lightly buttered. Pre-heat the oven to gas mark 6, 400°F (200°C).

Begin by toasting all the pecan nuts. Place them on a baking tray and bake in the oven for 7 minutes until lightly toasted or, if you watch them like a hawk, you can toast them under a grill. Then chop them quite small.

Place the biscuits in a bowl and crush them with the base of a rolling pin. Add the melted butter and half the nuts, mix them well then press all this into the base of the cake tin and pre-bake the base in the oven for 15 minutes. Then lower the temperature to gas mark 2, 300°F (150°C).

For the filling, first blend the bananas and lemon juice in a food processor until smooth, then simply add all the rest of the filling ingredients. Blend again then pour it all over the biscuit base and bake on the middle shelf of the oven for 1 hour. Turn off the oven and leave the cheesecake inside to cool slowly until completely cold; this slow cooling will stop the cheesecake cracking.

To make the sauce, place the butter, sugars and syrup in a saucepan and, over a very low heat, allow everything to dissolve completely. Let it cook for about 5 minutes. Pour in the cream and vanilla extract and stir until everything is smooth, then add the rest of the chopped pecan nuts. Remove it from the heat and allow it to cool completely before pouring it into a jug ready for serving.

When you are ready to assemble the cheesecake put the 2 tablespoons of lemon juice into a bowl. Slice the remaining bananas at an oblique angle into ¼-inch (5-mm) slices, and gently toss them around to get an even coating of juice. If you like you can spoon a small circle of sauce into the centre, then layer the bananas in overlapping circles all round it. Serve the cheesecake cut into slices with the rest of the sauce handed round separately.

Banoffee Cheesecake with Toffee Pecan Sauce

Tiramisu

T*here isn't a classic recipe for Tiramisu as such, as there are many varying versions both in Italy and around the world, but the following one is I think the nicest I've come across. For lovers of strong coffee, dark chocolate and the rich creaminess of Mascarpone it is one of the nicest, easiest and most popular desserts of the party season.*

3 x size 1 egg yolks
2 oz (50 g) caster sugar
1 x 250 g tub Mascarpone (Italian cream cheese)
2 x size 1 egg whites
5 fl oz (150 ml) very strong espresso coffee
3 tablespoons dark rum

About 24 sponge fingers (or boudoir biscuits)
2 oz (50 g) dark continental chocolate, with 75% cocoa solids, chopped
1 level dessertspoon/tablespoon cocoa powder

You will also need 6 stemmed glasses, approximately 7-fl oz (200-ml) capacity.

First put the egg yolks into a medium-sized bowl together with the sugar and beat with an electric hand whisk on high speed for about 3 minutes or until the mixture forms a light, pale mousse. In a separate large bowl stir the Mascarpone with a wooden spoon to soften it, then gradually beat in the egg yolk mixture. Between each addition beat well until the mixture is smooth before adding more. Now wash and dry the beaters of the whisk so they are perfectly clean, then in a third separate bowl whisk the egg whites until they form soft peaks. Now lightly fold this into the Mascarpone mixture and then put the bowl to one side.

Next break the biscuits in half, then pour the coffee and rum into a shallow dish and then dip the sponge fingers briefly into it, turning them over – they will absorb the liquid very quickly. Now simply layer the desserts by putting 3 of the soaked sponge halves into each glass, followed by a tablespoon of Mascarpone mixture and a layer of chopped chocolate. Repeat the whole process, putting 5 halves in next, followed by the Mascarpone, finishing with a layer of chopped chocolate and a final dusting of cocoa powder. Cover the glasses with clingfilm then chill in the refrigerator for several hours and serve straight from the fridge – I think it tastes better very cold.

———————————◇———————————

Tiramisu

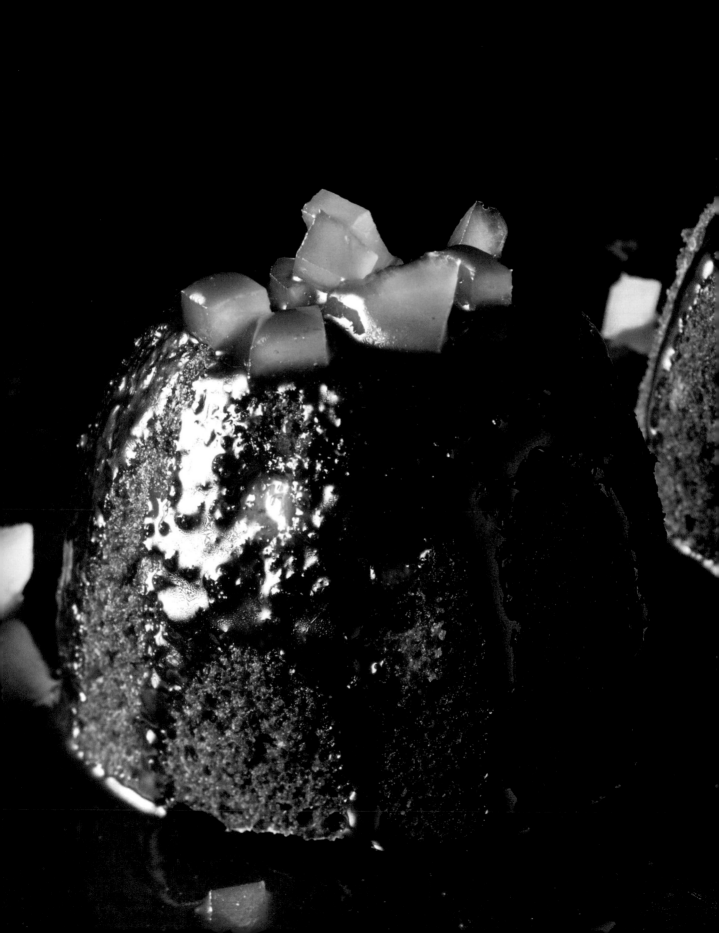

Chocolate Bread and Butter Pudding

SERVES 6

I have to thank Larkin Warren for her original recipe from her restaurant, Martha's Vineyard, which I have adapted. It is quite simply one of the most brilliant hot puddings ever invented. It's so simple but so good – and even better prepared two days in advance. Serve in small portions because it is very rich. Though I doubt if there will be any left over, it's also wonderful cold.

9 slices, each ¼ inch (5 mm) thick, good quality white bread, 1 day old, taken from a large loaf

5 oz (150 g) dark continental chocolate with 75% cocoa solids

15 fl oz (425 ml) whipping cream

4 tablespoons dark rum

4 oz (110 g) caster sugar

3 oz (75 g) butter

A good pinch cinnamon

3 x size 1 eggs

TO SERVE:
Double cream, well chilled

You will also need a shallow ovenproof dish 7 x 9 inches (18 x 23 cm) base x 2 inches (5 cm) deep, lightly buttered.

Begin by removing the crusts from the slices of bread, which should leave you with approximately 9 x 4-inch (10-cm) squares. So now cut each slice into 4 triangles. Next place the chocolate, whipping cream, rum, sugar, butter and cinnamon in a bowl set over a saucepan of barely simmering water, being careful not to let the bowl touch the water, then wait until the butter and chocolate have melted and the sugar has completely dissolved. Next remove the bowl from the heat and give it a really good stir to amalgamate all the ingredients.

Now in a separate bowl, whisk the eggs and then pour the chocolate mixture over them and whisk again very thoroughly to blend them together.

Then spoon about a ½-inch (1-cm) layer of the chocolate mixture into the base of the dish and arrange half the bread triangles over the chocolate in overlapping rows. Now pour half the remaining chocolate mixture all over the bread as evenly as possible then arrange the rest of the triangles over that, finishing off with a layer of chocolate. Use a fork to press the bread gently down so that it gets covered very evenly with the liquid as it cools.

Cover the dish with clingfilm and allow to stand at room temperature for 2 hours before transferring it to the fridge for a minimum of 24 (but preferably 48) hours before cooking. When you're ready to cook the pudding, pre-heat the oven to gas mark 4, 350°F (180°C). Remove the clingfilm and bake in the oven on a high shelf for 30-35 minutes, by which time the top will be crunchy and the inside soft and squidgey. Leave it to stand for 10 minutes before serving with well-chilled double cream poured over.

───────── ◇ ─────────

Chocolate Bread and Butter Pudding

Hot Cross Buns

MAKES 12

Hot cross buns cannot be dashed off quickly — they are best made when you have set aside some time to lock yourself in the kitchen, switch on the radio and lose yourself in a rewarding session of yeast cookery. Kneading the dough and watching it rise is all very satisfying, and then your family can enjoy all that fruity, spicy stickiness! Hot cross buns are a special occasion in themselves, so serve them still slightly warm from the oven and spread with best butter.

1 lb (450 g) strong plain white flour
1 level teaspoon salt
1 level teaspoon mixed spice
½ teaspoon cinnamon
½ teaspoon freshly grated nutmeg
2 x 6 g sachets easy-blend yeast
2 oz (50 g) caster sugar
4 oz (110 g) currants
2 oz (50 g) chopped mixed peel
5 fl oz (150 ml) hand-hot milk
1½–2 fl oz (40–55 ml) warmed water
1 x size 1 egg, beaten

2 oz (50 g) butter, melted
FOR THE CROSSES:
2 oz (50 g) plain flour
1½ tablespoons water
FOR THE GLAZE:
2 tablespoons granulated sugar
2 tablespoons water

You will also need a greased baking sheet and a large polythene bag, lightly oiled.

First of all sift the flour, salt, mixed spice, cinnamon and nutmeg into a mixing bowl. Then sprinkle in the yeast and caster sugar, followed by the currants and mixed peel. Mix everything together evenly. Then make a well in the centre and pour in the milk and water, followed by the beaten egg and melted butter.

Now mix everything to a dough, starting off with a wooden spoon and then using your hands when the mixture becomes less sticky. Because it is never possible to be exact with the liquid, as flour can vary, if you need to add a spot more water, do so — or if you find the mixture is getting too sticky, sprinkle in a bit more flour.

Then transfer the dough to a clean surface and knead it until it feels smooth and elastic — this will take about 6 minutes. After that place the dough back in the bowl and cover the bowl with clingfilm. Leave it in a warm place to rise — it will take about 1½ hours to double in size. If it takes longer than that, don't worry, just wait until the dough is double its original volume. Then, pressing the air out of it, reshape the dough.

Now divide it into 12 round portions and place them on the greased baking sheet, leaving plenty of room around each one. Use a sharp knife to make a cross on the top of each bun. Then leave them to rise again, covering them with an oiled polythene bag. This time they will take about 30 minutes.

While that's happening, pre-heat the oven to gas mark 7, 425°F (220°C) and make the crosses. Form a paste with the flour and water, then roll this out and cut it into ¼-inch (5-mm) strips. When the second rising time is up, brush the strips with water to make them stick and place them on top of the buns along the

BACK *TO* HOME BAKING

indentations you made earlier. Put the buns on a high shelf in the oven and bake them for about 15 minutes.

While they are cooking, make the glaze by slowly melting together the sugar and water over a gentle heat until all the sugar grains have dissolved and you have a clear syrup. As soon as the buns come out of the oven, brush them immediately with the glaze while they are still warm. If you want to make them ahead of time, it's quite nice just to warm them through again in the oven before eating. If you want to freeze them, they do freeze well – just remember to put on the glaze after defrosting and then warm the buns through in the oven.

———————————◇———————————

Four Nut Chocolate Brownies

*I*f *you've never made brownies before, you first need to get into the brownie mode, and to do this stop thinking 'cakes'. Brownies are slightly crisp on the outside but soft, damp and squidgey within. I'm always getting letters from people who think their brownies are not cooked, so once you've accepted the description above, try and forget all about cakes.*

2 oz (50 g) dark continental chocolate, with 75% cocoa solids
4 oz (110 g) butter
2 x size 1 eggs, beaten
8 oz (225 g) granulated sugar
2 oz (50 g) plain flour
1 level teaspoon baking powder
¼ teaspoon salt

1 oz (25 g) each macadamia, brazil, pecan and hazelnuts

You will also need a well-greased oblong tin measuring 7 x 11 inches (18 x 28 cm), lined with baking parchment, allowing the paper to come 1 inch (2.5 cm) above the tin. Pre-heat the oven to gas mark 4, 350°F (180°C).

Begin by chopping the nuts roughly, not too small, then place them on a baking sheet and toast them in a pre-heated oven for 8 minutes exactly. Please use a timer here otherwise you'll be throwing burned nuts away all day! While the nuts are cooking, put the chocolate and butter together in a large mixing bowl fitted over a saucepan of barely simmering water, making sure the bowl doesn't touch the water. Allow the chocolate to melt, then beat it until smooth, remove it from the heat and simply stir in all the other ingredients until thoroughly blended.

Now spread the mixture evenly into the prepared tin and bake on the centre shelf of the oven for 30 minutes or until it's slightly springy in the centre. Remove the tin from the oven and leave it to cool for 10 minutes before cutting into roughly 15 squares. Then, using a palette knife, transfer the squares onto a wire rack to finish cooling.

———————◇———————

Four Nut Chocolate Brownies

Iced Lemon Curd Layer Cake

*Y*ou couldn't get a more lemony recipe than this: layers of lemon-flavoured sponge, filled with home-made lemon curd and then a lemon icing for the finishing touch. It's wonderful.

6 oz (175 g) self-raising flour, sifted	**2 x size 1 eggs**
1 level teaspoon baking powder	**2 oz (50 g) unsalted butter**
6 oz (175 g) butter at room temperature	
6 oz (175 g) caster sugar	FOR THE ICING:
3 x size 1 eggs	**2 oz (50 g) sifted icing sugar**
Grated rind of 1 lemon	**Zest of 1 large lemon**
1 tablespoon lemon juice	**2–3 teaspoons lemon juice**

FOR THE LEMON CURD:

3 oz (75 g) caster sugar

Grated zest and juice of 1 large juicy lemon

Prepare 2 x 7-inch (18-cm) sandwich tins, 1½ inches (4 cm) deep, by greasing them, lining the bases with greaseproof or silicone paper and greasing the paper too.

Pre-heat the oven to gas mark 3, 325°F (170°C).

Just measure all the cake ingredients into a mixing bowl and beat – ideally with an electric hand whisk – till you have a smooth, creamy consistency. Then divide the mixture evenly between the two tins and bake them on the centre shelf of the oven for about 35 minutes or until the centres feel springy when lightly touched with a little finger.

While the cakes are cooking, make the lemon curd. Place the sugar and grated lemon rind in a bowl, whisk the lemon juice together with the eggs, then pour this over the sugar. Then add the butter cut into little pieces, and place the bowl over a pan of barely simmering water. Stir frequently till thickened – about 20 minutes. You don't have to stay with it – just come back from time to time to give it a stir.

When the cakes are cooked, remove them from the oven and after about 30 seconds turn them out onto a wire rack. When they are absolutely cold – and not before – carefully cut each one horizontally into 2, using a sharp serrated knife. Now spread the curd thickly to sandwich the sponges together.

Then to make the icing, begin by removing the zest from the lemon – it's best to use a zester to get long, curly strips. Then sift the icing sugar into a bowl and gradually stir in the lemon juice until you have a soft, runny consistency. Allow the icing to stand for 5 minutes before spreading it on top of the cake with a knife, almost to the edges, and don't worry if it runs a little down the sides of the cake. Then scatter the lemon zest over the top and leave it for half an hour for the icing to firm up before serving.

———————◇———————

Iced Lemon Curd Layer Cake